**ROUGH
GUIDES**

POCKET **ROUGH GUIDE**
DUBAI

Withdrawn

PLACES

View of Burj Al Arab from Madinat Jumeirah

Bur Dubai

Strung out along the southern side of the Creek, Bur Dubai is the oldest part of the city. Parts of the district's historic waterfront still retain their engagingly old-fashioned appearance, with a tangle of sand-coloured buildings and a distinctively Arabian skyline, spiked with wind towers and the occasional minaret. At the heart of the district, the absorbing Dubai Museum offers an excellent introduction to the city's history, while the old Iranian quarter of Bastakiya (also known as the Al Fahidi Historical Neighbourhood) is home to an impressive collection of traditional buildings. Heading west along the Creek, the old-fashioned Textile Souk is the prettiest in the city, while to the north the historic quarter of Shindagha is home to a fine cluster of century-old edifices.

The Creek

MAP P.26, POCKET MAP M11–N10

Cutting a broad, salty swathe through the middle of the city centre, **the Creek** (Al Khor in Arabic) lies physically and historically at the very heart of Dubai. The Creek was the location of the earliest settlements in the area – first on the Bur Dubai side of the water, and subsequently in Deira – and also played a crucial role in establishing Dubai as a major port during the twentieth century. Commerce aside, the Creek remains the centrepiece of Dubai and its finest natural feature; a broad, serene stretch of water which is as essential a part of the fabric and texture of the city as the

The Creek

Thames is to London or the Seine to Paris.

The walk along the Bur Dubai waterfront is particularly lovely, pedestrianized throughout, and with cooling breezes and wonderful views of the city down the Creek – particularly beautiful towards sunset. For the best views, begin in Shindagha (see page 29) and head south; it takes about 20–25 minutes to reach Bastakiya. A spacious promenade stretches down the waterfront as far as Shindagha Tower, from where a narrow walkway extends down to the Bur Dubai Abra Station and the Textile Souk.

Dubai Museum

MAP P.26, POCKET MAP M12
Al Fahidi St. Al Fahidi metro ☏ 04 353 1862, Ⓦ tinyurl.com/DubaiMus. Sat–Thurs 8.30am–8.30pm, Fri 2.30–8.30pm. 3dh.

At the dead centre of Bur Dubai stands the old **Al Fahidi Fort**, a rough-and-ready little structure whose engagingly lopsided corner turrets – one square and one round – make it look a bit like a giant sandcastle. Dating from around 1800, the fort is the oldest building in Dubai, having originally been built to defend the town's landward approaches against raids by rival Bedouin tribes; it also served as the residence and office of the ruling sheikh up until the early twentieth century before being converted into a museum in 1971.

The fort now provides a home for the excellent **Dubai Museum**, a logical first stop on any tour of the city and the perfect place to get up to speed with the history and culture of the emirate. Entering the museum you step into the fort's central **courtyard**, dotted with assorted wooden boats revealing the different types of vessel used in old Dubai, including a traditional abra, not so very different from those still in service on the Creek today (see page 29). In one corner stands a traditional *barasti* (or *areesh*) hut,

Dubai Museum

topped by a basic burlap wind tower – the sort of building most people in Dubai lived in right up until the 1960s. The hut's walls are made out of neatly cut palm branches, spaced so that breezes are able to blow right through and meaning it stays surprisingly cool even in the heat of the day.

The museum's real attraction, however, is its sprawling **underground section**, a buried wonderland which offers as comprehensive an overview of the traditional life, crafts and culture of Dubai as you'll find anywhere. A sequence of rooms – full of the sound effects and life-sized mannequins without which no Dubai museum would be complete – covers every significant aspect of traditional Dubaian life, including Islam, local architecture and wind towers, traditional dress and games, camels and falconry. Interesting short films on various subjects are shown in many of the rooms, including fascinating historic footage of pearl divers at work. There's also a line of shops featuring a range of traditional trades and crafts – carpenters, blacksmiths,

Bur Dubai

SHINDAGHA

Crossroads of
Civilizations
Museum

Sheikh Saeed
al Maktoum House

AL KHALEEJ ROAD

Shindagha
City Centre

AL GHUBAIBA ROAD

AL GHUBAIBA

Traditional
Architecture Museum

AL RAS

BANIYAS ROAD

Al Ghubaiba
Bus Station

Shindagha
Tower

DUBAI
FERRY

AL RAS

Heritage House

OLD BALADIYA RD

Al Ahmadiya
School

16TH STREET

AL FALAH ST

5 A STREET

BUR DUBAI
ABRA

AL RAS ROAD

Gold
Souk

21 A STREET

3 A STREET

ROLLA STREET

14 A STREET

17A STREET

AL RAFFA ST

AL NAHDA STREET

Textile Souk

BUR DUBAI
OLD SOUK ABRA

Grand
Souk Deira

KHALID BIN AL WALEED ROAD

AL RAFFA

Iranian Mosques

Spice Souk

16 A STREET

17 B STREET

19TH STREET

13TH STREET

9 B STREET

3 C ST

35TH STREET

37 D STREET

Hindi
Lane

DEIRA
OLD SOUK
ABRA

ROLLA STREET

Grand
Mosque

24 B STREET

HISN STREET

AL FAHIDI

Dubai
Museum

Diwan

Diwan
Mosque

Al Rais
Centre

Al Khaleej
Centre

41 ST STREET

60 B ST

BASTAKIYA

Dhow
Wharfage

AL MANKHOOL ROAD

AL FAHIDI
ROUNDABOUT

SMCCU
Majlis
Gallery

AL SABKHA
ABRA

Al Ain
Centre

AL MUSSALLA ROAD

AL FAHIDI

The Creek

4 A STREET

8 A STREET

10 A ST

6TH STREET

9TH STREET

13 A STREET

124
84

15 A STREET

7TH STREET

3 A STREET

16 A STREET

18TH STREET

17TH ST

AL HAMRIYA

12 A STREET

16 A STREET

GOLDEN SANDS

1 B STREET

16TH STREET

15 B ST

UK
Embassy

15 B STREET

13 C STREET

17 B STREET

22 A STREET

11 B ST

20TH STREET

26 A STREET

28 A STREET

Wonder
Bus

BurJuman
@

26 B STREET

BURJUMAN

Spinneys

SHEIKH KHALIFA BIN ZAYED ST

2ND STREET

US
Consulate

2 B STREET

BIN ZAYED STREET

2 A STREET

4TH STREET

4 A STREET

6TH STREET

4 B STREET

11TH STREET

6 A STREET

KARAMA

1ST STREET

KHALID BIN AL WALEED ROAD

8 C ST

8TH STREET

3RD STREET

AL SEEF ROAD

AL SEEF
ABRA

10 B STREET

18 A ST

124
77

12 B STREET

Karama Centre

124
84

ZA'ABEEL ROAD

24TH ST

7 B STREET

UMM HURAIR 1

3 B STREET

28TH ST

The Creek

UMM HURAIR ROAD

MAKTOUM BRIDGE

Dubai
TV & Radio

124
76

Dubai
Courts

SHOPS

Ajmal	4
Bateel Dates	4
BurJuman	4
Carrefour	1
Dream Girl Tailors	3
International	
Aladdin Shoes	2

CAFÉS

Arabian Tea House Café	6
Bayt al Wakeel	3
Dôme	8
XVA Café	5

RESTAURANTS

Antique Bazaar	7
Barjeel al Arab	1
Bastakiah Nights	4
Vasanta Bhavan	2

BARS

Sherlock Holmes	1
Viceroy Bar	2

ACCOMMODATION

Arabian Courtyard	3
Barjeel Heritage	
Guest House	1
Four Points Sheraton	
Bur Dubai	6
Orient Guest House	5
Time Palace Hotel	2
XVA	4

Wind towers

Often described as the world's oldest form of air-conditioning, the distinctive **wind towers** (*barjeel*) that top many old Dubai buildings (as well as numerous modern ones constructed in faux-Arabian style) provided an ingeniously simple way of countering the Gulf's searing temperatures in a pre-electrical age. Rising around 6m above the rooftops on which they're built, wind towers are open on all four sides and channel any available breezes down into the building via triangular flues. Bastakiya's collection of wind towers is the largest and finest in the city, with subtle variations in design from tower to tower, meaning that no two are ever exactly alike.

tailors, spice merchants and so on. It's kitsch but undeniably engaging, populated with colourful mannequins in traditional dress, although the old black-and-white video clips of artisans at work add a slightly spooky touch.

Bastakiya
MAP P.26, POCKET MAP N12
Al Fahidi metro. Coins Museum Sun–Thurs 8am–2pm & 5–8pm. Coffee Museum ⓦ coffeemuseum.ae; Sat–Thurs 9am–5pm. Architectural Heritage Department Sun–Thurs 8am–2pm. Majlis Gallery ⓣ 04 353 6233, ⓦ themajlisgallery.com; Sat–Thurs 10am–6pm (June & July till 2pm).
The beautiful old quarter of **Bastakiya** (also know as the **Al Fahidi Historical Neighbourhood**) comprises a photogenic huddle of traditional Gulf houses, capped with dozens of wind towers and arranged around a rabbit warren of tiny alleyways. A number of old Bastakiya houses have now been opened to the public as small-scale museums and galleries. Best is the quaint little **Coffee Museum**, stuffed full of antique coffee-making paraphernalia and other artefacts from around the world. Also worth a look are the **Coins Museum**, containing a well-presented collection of Islamic coins, and the **Architectural Heritage Department**, boasting a particularly large and chintzy courtyard and fine views over Bastakiya from its roof. Nearby is the long-running **Majlis Gallery**,

the oldest in the city, founded in 1989 and hosting monthly exhibitions showcasing the work of Emirati and international artists.

The SMCCU
MAP P.26, POCKET MAP N12
Near Al Fahidi Roundabout. Al Fahidi metro ⓣ 04 353 6666, ⓦ cultures.ae. Sun–Thurs 8am–4pm, Sat 9am–1pm.
Based in an office on the eastern edge of Bastakiya, the pioneering **Sheikh Mohammed Centre for Cultural Understanding**, or **SMCCU**, runs popular tours of Jumeirah Mosque (see page 60) and a number of activities in Bastakiya itself, including **walking tours**, Gulf Arabic classes and "cultural" breakfasts and lunches, during which you get the chance to sample some traditional food while chatting to the centre's Emirati staff.

The Grand Mosque and Diwan
MAP P.26, POCKET MAP M11 & N12
Next to the Al Fahidi Fort, Ali bin Abi Taleb St. Al Fahidi metro. No entry to non-Muslims.
The biggest in Dubai, the imposing **Grand Mosque** is an impressively large if rather plain structure, the general austerity relieved only by an elaborate swirl of Koranic script over the entrance and the city's tallest minaret. Hugging the creekside immediately east of the Grand Mosque sits the **Diwan**, or Ruler's Court, now home to

Textile Souk

assorted government functionaries, and the eye-catching **Diwan Mosque**, topped by an unusually flattened onion dome and a slender white minaret which rivals that of the nearby Grand Mosque in height.

The Textile Souk

MAP P.26, POCKET MAP M11
Al Ghubaiba metro.

At the heart of Bur Dubai, the **Textile Souk** (also sometimes referred to as the "Old Souk") is easily the prettiest in the city, occupying an immaculately restored traditional bazaar, its long line of sand-coloured buildings shaded by a fine arched wooden roof, pleasantly cool even in the heat of the day and illuminated by traditional Moorish hanging lights after dark. This was once the most important bazaar in the city although its commercial importance has long since faded and almost all the shops have now been taken over by Indian traders flogging reams of sari cloth and fluorescent blankets, alongside assorted tourist tat (if you're hankering for an I LOVE DUBAI T-shirt or spangly camel, now's your chance).

Hindi Lane

MAP P.26, POCKET MAP M11
Textile Souk. Al Fahidi metro.

The colourful little alleyway popularly known as **Hindi Lane** is one of Dubai's most curious and appealing little ethnic enclaves. Walk to the far (eastern) end of the Textile Souk, turn right by T. Singh Trading and then left by Shubham Textiles and you'll find yourself in a tiny alleyway lined with picturesque little Indian shops selling an array of bangles, bindis, coconuts, flowers, bells, almanacs and other religious paraphernalia. On the north side of Hindi Lane is the tiny hybridized Hindu-cum-Sikh temple sometimes referred to as the **Sikh Gurudaba**, while continuing along Hindi Lane to the back of the Grand Mosque brings you to a second Hindu temple, the **Shri Nathji Temple**, dedicated to Krishna.

Iranian mosques

MAP P.26, POCKET MAP M11
Ali bin Abi Taleb St (11c St). Al Ghubaiba

metro. No entry to non-Muslims.

Hidden away on the south side of the Textile Souk are two of the city's finest **Iranian mosques**. The more easterly of the two mosques is particularly eye-catching, with a superb facade and dome covered in a lustrous mosaic of predominantly blue tiling decorated with geometrical floral motifs. The second mosque, about 50m west along the road, close to the *Time Palace Hotel*, is a contrastingly plain, sand-coloured building, its rooftop enlivened by four tightly packed little egg-shaped domes.

Al Fahidi Street

MAP P.26, POCKET MAP M11–N12
Al Fahidi and BurJuman metros.
Al Fahidi Street is Bur Dubai's de facto high street, lined with a mix of shops selling Indian clothing, shoes and jewellery along with other places stacked high with mobile phones and fancy watches (not necessarily genuine). The eastern end of the street and adjacent Al Hisn Street are also often loosely referred to as **Meena Bazaar**, the centre of the district's textile and tailoring industry and home to a dense razzle-dazzle of shopfronts stuffed with sumptuous saris.

Shindagha

MAP P.26, POCKET MAP M10–N10

Although now effectively swallowed up by Bur Dubai, the historic creekside district of **Shindagha** was, until fifty years ago, a quite separate and self-contained area occupying its own spit of land, and frequently cut off from Bur Dubai proper during high tides. This was once the most exclusive address in town, home to the ruling family and other local elites, who occupied a series of imposing houses lined up along the waterfront. The edge of the district is guarded by the distinctive waterfront **Shindagha Tower**, instantly recognizable thanks to the slit windows and protruding buttress on each side, arranged to resemble a human face.

Sheikh Saeed al Maktoum House

MAP P.26, POCKET MAP M10
Shindagha waterfront. Al Ghubaiba metro
🛈 04 226 0286. Closed for renovation at the time of writing.
Standing on the beautiful Shindagha waterfront, the **Sheikh Saeed al Maktoum House** is one of Dubai's most interesting museums, occupying what from 1896 to 1958 was the principal residence of Dubai's ruling family – an atmospheric wind-towered mansion arranged around a spacious sandy courtyard. Inside, pride of place goes to the superb collection of old **photographs**,

Crossing the Creek by abra

One of the most fun things you can do in Bur Dubai is go for a ride by abra (see page 110) across the Creek – the area's two main abra stations are the **Bur Dubai Abra Station**, just outside the main entrance to the Textile Souk, and **Bur Dubai Old Souk Abra Station**, inside the souk itself, from where these old-fashioned little wooden boats shuttle across the Creek at all hours of the day and night to Deira Old Souk and Al Sabkha abra stations on the other side of the water in Deira. The boats' basic design has changed little for at least a century, apart from the addition of a diesel engine, and abras still play a crucial role in the city's transport infrastructure, carrying a staggering twenty million passengers per year for a modest 1dh per trip.

with images of the city from the 1940s through to the late 1960s, showing the first steps in its amazing transformation from a remote Gulf town to global megalopolis.

Traditional Architecture Museum

MAP P.26, POCKET MAP M10
Shindagha waterfront. Al Ghubaiba metro
☎ 04 353 1862, ⓦ bit.ly/TradArchMus.
Sun–Thurs 8am–2pm. Free.

One of the most interesting of the hotchpotch of Shindagha museums, the **Traditional Architecture Museum**, halfway between Shindagha Tower and Sheikh Saeed al Maktoum House, occupies a rather grand traditional house with the usual sandy courtyard, wind towers and elaborate latticed wall-panels decorated with geometrical and floral patterns. Inside, informative displays cover the story of architecture in the Emirates generally and Dubai in particular.

Crossroads of Civilizations Museum

MAP P.26, POCKET MAP M10
Al Khaleej Road. Al Ghubaiba Metro ☎ 04 393 4440, ⓦ themuseum.ae. Sat–Thurs 8am–8pm. 30dh.

Hidden away at the back of the Shindagha, this excellent museum showcases a small but spectacular array of mainly Middle Eastern artefacts. Highlights include some marvellously well-preserved Sumerian and Babylonian statuettes, and a superb piece of *kiswah* (the cloth used to cover the Ka'aba in Mecca) donated by the great Ottoman ruler Suleiman the Magnificent.

Traditional Architecture Museum courtyard

Shops

Ajmal

MAP P.26, POCKET MAP M3

BurJuman. BurJuman metro ☎ 04 351 5505, ⓦ ajmalperfume.com. Daily 9am–10pm (Thurs & Fri until 11pm). Dubai's leading perfumiers, offering a wide range of fragrances including traditional *attar*-based Arabian scents. If you don't like any of their ready-made perfumes you can make up your own from the big glass bottles on display behind the counter. Other branches are at Deira Gold Souk, Deira City Centre, Dubai Mall, Festival City and Mall of the Emirates.

Bateel Dates

MAP P.26, POCKET MAP M3

BurJuman. BurJuman metro ☎ 04 355 2853, ⓦ bateel.com. Daily 10am–10pm (Thurs & Fri until 11pm). The best dates in the city, grown in Bateel's own plantations in Saudi Arabia and sold either plain, covered in chocolate or stuffed with ingredients such as almonds and slices of lemon or orange. Other branches are at Deira City Centre, Festival Centre, Souk al Bahar and Dubai Mall.

BurJuman

MAP P.26, POCKET MAP M3

Corner of Khalid bin al Waleed and Sheikh Zayed roads. BurJuman metro (exit 3) ☎ 04 352 0222, ⓦ burjuman.com. Daily 10am–10pm (Thurs & Fri until 11pm). The biggest and best city-centre mall, BurJuman remains popular thanks to its convenient location and 300-plus shops, including the flagship Saks Fifth Avenue department store.

Carrefour

MAP P.26, POCKET MAP L10

Shindagha City Centre, Al Ghubaiba Rd. Al Ghubaiba metro ☎ 04 393 5601, ⓦ carrefouruae.com. Daily 9am–midnight. This vast French hypermarket chain might not be the most atmospheric

BurJuman

place to shop in the city, but is one of the best places to pick up just about any kind of Middle Eastern foodstuff you fancy, and is also a good source of cheap electronics and perfumes. Other branches are at Deira City Centre, Mall of the Emirates and Marina Mall.

Dream Girl Tailors

MAP P.26, POCKET MAP L12

37d Street. Al Fahidi metro ☎ 04 388 0070. Daily 10am–1pm & 4–10pm, Fri 6–9pm only. Perhaps the best of the various tailors hereabouts, offering well-made, inexpensive copies of any existing garment you might bring in: around 75dh for a shirt or trousers, or from 200dh for a dress (not including material). They can also make up clothes from photographs or even a hand-drawn design.

International Aladdin Shoes

MAP P.26, POCKET MAP M11

Textile Souk (next to Bur Dubai Old Souk Abra Station). Al Ghubaiba metro ☎ 050 744 6543. Daily 9am–10pm. Eye-catching little stall (no sign) in the midst of the Textile Souk selling a gorgeous selection of colourful embroidered ladies' slippers (from 50dh) along with lovely embroidered belts.

Cafés

Arabian Tea House Café

MAP P.26, POCKET MAP N12

Al Fahidi St, next to the main entrance to Bastakiya. Al Fahidi metro ☎ 04 353 5071, Ⓦ arabianteahouse.co. Daily 8am–10pm.

Lovely little courtyard café set in the idyllic garden of a traditional old Bastakiya house. The menu features a good range of sandwiches and salads (from 35dh), plus assorted Arabian-style breakfasts and mains (50–60dh) and a good choice of juices and coffees.

Bayt Al Wakeel

MAP P.26, POCKET MAP M11

Mackenzie House, near the main entrance to the Textile Souk. Al Ghubaiba metro ☎ 04 353 0530, Ⓦ wakeel.ae. Daily 11am–midnight.

The small menu of rather pedestrian Arabian food (plus some pricier seafood options) won't win any awards, but the convenient location near the entrance to the Textile Souk and the setting by the historic Mackenzie House on an attractive terrace jutting out

into the Creek amply compensate. Mezze from 15dh, mains 36–80dh.

Dôme

MAP P.26, POCKET MAP M3

BurJuman. BurJuman metro ☎ 04 355 6004, Ⓦ domecafes.ae. Daily 8am–10pm.

This low-key café is a reliable source of good coffee and cheap grub including pasta, pizzas, soups, salads, burgers and a few more substantial international mains, plus very competitively priced daily specials, with mains for around 40–56dh. Other branches at DIFC, Dubai Mall, Jumaira Plaza, Souk Madinat Jumeirah and the Al Ghurair Centre.

Geewin Cafe

MAP P.36, POCKET MAP N11

Creekside, near Deira Old Souq Abra Station

This little kiosk, next to where the boats leave to cross the channel, takes its name from a pearl of the highest quality. *Geewin's* produce is also quite unique – it sells ice cream made exclusively from camel milk. Choose from flavours such as saffron or datem or more well-known tastes like pistachio or hazelnut. A bowl of ice cream will cost you around 20dh.

XVA Café

MAP P.26, POCKET MAP N12

Arabian Tea House Café

Bastakiya. Al Fahidi metro ☏ 04 353 5383, Ⓦ xvahotel.com. Daily 7am–10pm.

Tucked away in an alley at the back of Bastakiya, this shady courtyard café (attached to a lovely guesthouse; see page 99) serves up good meat-free meals including flavoursome salads and sandwiches (35–40dh) and assorted light meals (40–50dh) with a Middle Eastern twist – couscous with pomegranate and halloumi, for example, or beetroot kebab with roasted carrot – plus good breakfasts.

Restaurants

Antique Bazaar

MAP P.26, POCKET MAP M13
Four Points Sheraton, Khalid bin al Waleed Rd. Al Fahidi metro ☏ 04 397 7444, Ⓦ antiquebazaar-dubai.com. Daily 12.30–3pm & 7.30pm–2.30am, closed Fri lunch.

This pretty little restaurant, littered with assorted subcontinental artefacts, dishes up a fair selection of North Indian favourites with reasonable aplomb. There's also a decent resident band and dancers nightly from 9pm. Mains from around 45dh (veg), 60dh (meat).

Barjeel Al Arab

MAP P.26, POCKET MAP M10
Barjeel Heritage Guest House, Shindagha waterfront. Al Ghubaiba metro ☏ 04 354 4424, Ⓦ heritagedubaihotels.com. Daily noon–midnight.

There's plenty of old-school Arabian atmosphere in this appealing restaurant, set in a traditional house right on the Shindagha waterfront. The Middle Eastern menu (mains 40–70dh) includes local specialities, and it's also a good place for a camel burger or steak. No alcohol.

Bastakiah Nights

MAP P.26, POCKET MAP N12
Bastakiya. Al Fahidi metro ☏ 04 353 7772, Ⓦ facebook.com (search for "Bastakiah N Rest"). Daily 12.30–3pm & 6.30pm–midnight.

One of the more attractive places to eat in Bur Dubai, with indoor and courtyard seating in an attractively restored traditional house – although the short and overpriced Middle Eastern menu (mains 70–80dh) doesn't quite live up to the setting. No alcohol.

Vasanta Bhavan

MAP P.26, POCKET MAP L11
Vasantam Hotel, Al Nahda St. Al Ghubaiba or Al Fahidi metros ☏ 04 239 1177, Ⓦ thevasantabhavan.com. Daily 7am–11.30pm.

This cosy vegetarian establishment is one of the best of the hundreds of little curry houses dotted around Bur Dubai. Food is served in a comfortable and peaceful upstairs dining room, with an excellent range of North and South Indian standards (mains 7–12dh), richly flavoured and at giveaway prices.

Bars

Sherlock Holmes

MAP P.26, POCKET MAP M12
Arabian Courtyard Hotel, Al Fahidi St. Al Fahidi metro ☏ 04 351 9111, Ⓦ sherlockholmespub.net. Daily noon–3am (no alcohol served 4–6pm).

One of the better pubs hereabouts, with a relaxed atmosphere, flock wallpaper and glass cases full of vaguely Sherlock Holmes-related memorabilia – although noisy live music sometimes intrudes. Also does decent pub food.

Viceroy Bar

MAP P.26, POCKET MAP M13
Four Points Sheraton Hotel, Khalid bin al Waleed Rd. Al Fahidi metro ☏ 04 397 7444. Daily 12.30pm–2pm.

This traditional English-style pub is one of the nicest in Bur Dubai, complete with fake oak-beamed ceiling, authentic wooden bar and oodles of comfy leather armchairs.

Deira

North of the Creek lies Deira, the second of the old city's two principal districts, founded in 1841, when settlers from Bur Dubai crossed the Creek to establish a new village here. Deira rapidly overtook its older neighbour in commercial importance and remains notably more built-up and cosmopolitan than Bur Dubai, with a heady ethnic mix of Emiratis, Gulf Arabs, Iranians, Indians, Pakistanis and Somalis thronging its packed streets. Specific tourist attractions are thinner on the ground here than in Bur Dubai, but the district remains the best place in Dubai for aimless wandering, and even the shortest exploration will uncover a kaleidoscopic jumble of cultures, from Indian curry houses and Iranian grocers to Somali shisha cafés and backstreet mosques – not to mention an endless array of shops selling everything from formal black *abbeya* to belly-dancing costumes.

Gold Souk

MAP P.36, POCKET MAP N11
Between Sikkat al Khail Rd and Old Baladiya Rd. Al Ras metro. Most shops open around 10am–10pm.

Deira's famous **Gold Souk** is usually the first stop for visitors to the district, with over three hundred shops lined up along its wooden-roofed main arcade, their windows packed with a staggering quantity of jewellery – it's been estimated that there are usually around ten tonnes of gold here at any one time. The souk's main attraction is price: the gold available here is among the cheapest in the world, and massive competition keeps prices keen. Though the gold industry in Dubai is carefully regulated, with the daily gold price fixed in all shops citywide, you should always **bargain**. A request for "best price" or "small discount" should yield an immediate discount of around 20–25 percent, although it always pays to shop around. The jewellery on offer ranges from restrained European-style pieces to ornate Arabian creations – the traditional Emirati bracelets, fashioned from solid gold and hung in long lines in shop windows, are particularly appealing.

Heritage House

MAP P.36, POCKET MAP N11
Old Baladiya Rd. Al Ras metro. Closed for renovation at the time of writing.

One of the city's oldest museums, the engaging **Heritage House** offers the most complete picture of everyday life in old Dubai you'll find anywhere in town. The building (originally constructed in 1890) is a classic example of a traditional Gulf mansion, with rooms arranged around a large sandy courtyard. Each of the rooms is enlivened with exhibits evoking aspects of traditional Emirati life, along with a large cast of elaborately dressed mannequins going about their daily business: drinking coffee, spinning thread, grinding spices and so on, while a couple of waxwork children look incuriously on.

Al Ahmadiya School

MAP P.36, POCKET MAP N11
Old Baladiya Rd, next to the Heritage
House. Al Ras metro. Closed for renovation
at the time of writing.

Founded in 1912 by pearl
merchant Sheikh Mohammed
bin Ahmed bin Dalmouk, the **Al
Ahmadiya School** is one of the
city's finest surviving examples of
traditional Emirati architecture.
Al Ahmadiya was the first public
school in UAE, and many of the
city's leaders studied here – it
was also notably egalitarian,
with only the sons of wealthy
families being expected to pay.
Inside, a few modest exhibits
explore the educational history
of the emirate, with old photos
and the inevitable mannequins,
including three tiny pupils being
instructed by a rather irritable-
looking teacher brandishing a
wooden cane.

Grand Souk Deira

MAP P.36, POCKET MAP N11
Between Al Ras and Baniyas roads. Al
Ras metro. Most shops open around
10am–10pm, although some may close
around 1–4/5pm, and also on Fri mornings.

The extensive covered souk
formerly known as Al Souk
al Kabeer ("The Big Souk")
was once the largest and most
important market in Deira. Now
rechristened **Grand Souk Deira**,
the whole area has been given a
major makeover, although most
of the shops remain rather dull.
Easily the most interesting part of
the souk is the diminutive **Spice
Souk** (signed "Herbs Market"),
perhaps the most atmospheric –
and certainly the most fragrant
– of the city's many bazaars. Run
almost exclusively by Iranian
traders, the shops here stock a wide
variety of culinary, medicinal and
cosmetic products, with tubs of
merchandise set out in front of
each tiny shopfront, including great
piles of frankincense and other
exotic commodities.

Dhow Wharfage

MAP P.36, POCKET MAP N12
Deira creekside, between Deira Old Souk
and Al Sabkha abra stations. Al Ras metro.

The **Dhow Wharfage** offers
a fascinating glimpse into the
maritime traditions of old Dubai,
home to dozens of beautiful

Gold Souk

DEIRA

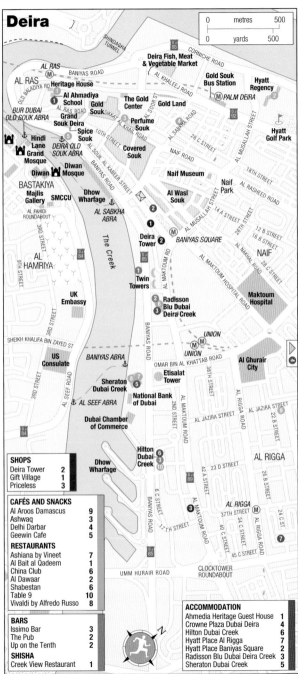

Deira

	metres	
0		500
0	yards	500

SHOPS

Deira Tower	2
Gift Village	1
Priceless	3

CAFÉS AND SNACKS

Al Aroos Damascus	9
Ashwaq	3
Delhi Darbar	4
Geewin Cafe	5

RESTAURANTS

Ashiana by Vineet	7
Al Bait al Qadeem	1
China Club	6
Al Dawaar	2
Shabestan	6
Table 9	10
Vivaldi by Alfredo Russo	8

BARS

Issimo Bar	3
The Pub	2
Up on the Tenth	2

SHISHA

Creek View Restaurant	1

ACCOMMODATION

Ahmedia Heritage Guest House	1
Crowne Plaza Dubai Deira	4
Hilton Dubai Creek	6
Hyatt Place Al Rigga	7
Hyatt Place Baniyas Square	2
Radisson Blu Dubai Deira Creek	3
Sheraton Dubai Creek	5

wooden dhows which berth here to load and unload cargo – hence the great tarpaulin-covered mounds of merchandise lying stacked up along the waterfront. The dhows themselves range in size from the fairly modest vessels employed for short hops up and down the coast to the large ocean-going craft used to transport goods around the Gulf and over to Iran, and even as far afield as Somalia, Pakistan and India. Virtually all of them fly the UAE flag, although they're generally manned by foreign crews who live on board.

Perfume Souk

MAP P.36, POCKET MAP O11
Sikkat al Khail Rd, immediately east of the Gold Souk. Al Ras metro. Most shops open around 10am–10pm, although some may close around 1–4/5pm, and also on Fri mornings.

Deira's **Perfume Souk** stretches along the western end of Sikkat al Khail Road, and also spills over into Al Soor and Souk Deira streets. Most of the shops here sell a mix of international brands (not necessarily genuine) along with the much heavier and more flowery oil-based *attar* perfumes favoured by local ladies. At many places you can also create your own scents, mixing and matching from the contents of the big bottles lined up behind the counter before taking them away in chintzy little cut-glass containers, many of which are collectibles in their own right.

Deira Fish, Meat and Vegetable Market

MAP P.36, POCKET MAP O10
Between Al Khaleej and Corniche roads. Palm Deira metro. No set hours, but usually busy from early in the morning until dark, or later.

The extensive **Deira Fish, Meat and Vegetable Market** occupies a large warehouse away from the hustle and bustle of central Deira; you can reach it by taking the footbridge over Al Khaleej Road opposite

Gold Land shopping centre. The fruit and vegetable section features a photogenic array of stalls piled high with rambutans, mangosteens, coconuts, vast watermelons, yams and a bewildering array of dates in huge, sticky piles. The less colourful – and far more malodorous – fish section is stocked with long lines of sharks, tuna and all sorts of other piscine species right down to sardines. There's also a small but rather gory meat section tucked away at the back.

Covered Souk

MAP P.36, POCKET MAP O11
Between Souk Deira St and Al Sabkha Rd. Al Ras metro. Shops open around 10am–10pm, although some may close around 1–4/5pm, and also on Fri mornings.

Deira's sprawling **Covered Souk** (a misnomer, since it isn't) comprises a rather indeterminate area of small shops arranged around the maze of narrow, pedestrianized alleyways which run south from Sikkat al Khail Road down towards the Creek. Most of the shops here are Indian-run, selling colourful, low-grade cloth for women's clothes, along with large quantities of mass-produced plastic

Dhow Wharfage

DEIRA

toys and cheap household goods. It's all rather down-at-heel, but makes for an interesting stroll, especially in the area at the back of the Al Sabkha bus station, the densest and busiest part of the bazaar, particularly after dark – expect to get lost at least once. The souk then continues, more or less unabated, on the far side of Al Sabkha Road, where it's known variously as the **Naif Souk** and **Al Wasl Souk**, before reaching Al Musallah Street.

Naif Museum

MAP P.36, POCKET MAP O2
Naif Police Station, Naif Fort, Sikkat al Khail Rd. Baniyas Square metro ☏ 04 227 6484, ⓦ tinyurl.com/NaifMus. Sun–Thurs 8am–2pm. Free.

Celebrating Dubai's formidable reputation for law and order, the modest **Naif Museum** lies tucked away in a corner of the imposing Naif Fort (originally built in 1939, but restored to death in 1997). It's actually a lot less tedious than you might fear, with mildly interesting exhibits on the history of law enforcement in the emirate from the foundation of the police force in 1956 (with just six officers under

a British captain) up to the present day. Exhibits include assorted old weapons and uniforms, various old photos and a trio of short films including some interesting historical footage.

The National Bank of Dubai and around

MAP P.36, POCKET MAP N3
Off Baniyas Rd immediately south of the Sheraton Dubai Creek Hotel. Union metro.

Next to the Creek in the southern part of Deira you'll find several of Dubai's original modernist landmarks. Pride of place goes to the **National Bank of Dubai** building (1998), its Creek-facing side covered by an enormous, curved sheet of highly polished glass, modelled on the sail of a traditional dhow. Next to the bank sits the shorter and squatter **Dubai Chamber of Commerce** (1995), an austerely minimalist glass-clad structure which seems to have been designed using nothing but triangles, while nearby on Omar bin al Khattab Road stands the **Etisalat Tower** (1986), instantly recognizable thanks to the enormous golf ball on its roof.

The National Bank of Dubai

Shops

Deira Tower

MAP P.36, POCKET MAP O13
Baniyas Square. Baniyas Square metro.
Most shops open 10am–9pm (although
many close around 2–4/5pm).

The so-called Deira Tower "Carpet
Souk" comprises thirty-odd stores
spread over two floors of a large
office block. Stock ranges from
huge, museum-quality Persian
heirlooms to ghastly framed carpet
pictures and other tat.

Gift Village

MAP P.36, POCKET MAP O12
Baniyas Square (next door to Hatam al
Tai café). Baniyas Square metro ☎ 04 294
6858, ⊕ tinyurl.com/GiftVillage. Sat–Thurs
9am–1am, Fri 9am–noon & 2pm–2am.

A veritable Aladdin's cave of
discounted everything, from pure
tat through to designer items,
including perfumes, electronics,
clothing, bags, sports equipment,
household appliances and
cuddly toys.

Priceless

MAP P.36, POCKET MAP O4
Al Maktoum Rd, near Deira Clock Tower.
Al Rigga metro ☎ 04 221 5444. Sat–Thurs
10am–10pm, Fri 2–10pm.

Worth the schlep for the excellent
spread of top designer menswear
and ladieswear – Armani, Yves
Saint-Laurent, Gucci and the like –
all sold at big discounts; two-thirds
off label prices is standard.

Cafés and snacks

Al Aroos Damascus

MAP P.36, POCKET MAP O3
Al Muraqqabat Rd. Al Rigga metro ☎ 04
221 9825, ⊕ aroosdamascus.com; Daily
7am–3am.

One of a number of lively local
Middle Eastern restaurants along Al
Muraqqabat Road – Dubai's "Little
Iraq" – and parallel Al Rigga Road.
All the usual Lebanese mezze and
grills are on offer – well cooked,
reasonably priced (mains from just
25dh) and served in huge portions.

Ashwaq

MAP P.36, POCKET MAP O11
Perfume Souk, Sikkat al Khail Rd. Al Ras
metro ☎ 04 226 1164. Sat–Thurs 8am–
midnight, Fri 3pm–midnight.

Close to the entrance to the
bustling Gold Souk, this is one
of the busiest and best of Deira's
various shwarma stands, with
melt-in-the-mouth shwarma
sandwiches (5dh) and big fruit
juices (from 10dh).

Delhi Darbar

MAP P.36, POCKET MAP O11
Al Sabkha Rd. Palm Deira metro ☎ 04 235
6161, ⊕ delhi-darbar.com. Daily 9am–2am.

Unpretentious but excellent
little no-frills restaurant serving
up heartwarming meat kebabs,
tandooris and Mughlai-style dishes
(from 24dh) along with a good
selection of veg curries (from 17dh)
and superb tandoori rotis at just
2dh a pop.

Restaurants

Ashiana by Vineet

MAP P.36, POCKET MAP N3
Sheraton Dubai Creek Hotel, Baniyas
Rd. Union metro ☎ 04 207 1733,
⊕ ashianadubai.com. Daily 7–11pm, plus
Sun–Thurs noon–3pm.

Long-running but consistently
popular Indian restaurant, now
overseen by masterchef Vineet
Bhatia and offering an interesting
selection of modern Indo-European
fusion dishes, alongside a few
subcontinental classics. Live music
at most meals. Mains 75–125dh.

Al Bait al Qadeem

MAP P.36, POCKET MAP N2
Old Baladiya Rd. Al Ras metro ☎ 04 225
6111, ⊕ albaitalqadeem.com. Daily
8am–10pm.

In a traditional building right next
to the Heritage House, with an

Al Aroos Damascus

attractive courtyard at the back and a pretty dining room. Food (mains 30–45dh) features well-prepared and reasonably-priced regional dishes along with more mainstream Lebanese-style kebabs.

China Club

MAP P.36, POCKET MAP O13
Radisson Blu Dubai Deira Creek Hotel, Baniyas Rd. Union metro ☏ 04 205 7033. Daily 12.30–3pm & 7.30–11pm.
The best Chinese restaurant in central Dubai, offering a daily "Yum Cha" buffet (99dh/139dh lunch/dinner) plus a good range of à la carte choices, including the restaurant's signature *dim sum* (34–44dh) and Peking duck. Most mains 70–110dh.

Al Dawaar

MAP P.36, POCKET MAP O1
Hyatt Regency, Corniche Rd. Palm Deira metro ☏ 04 209 6914. Sat–Wed 12.30-3.30pm & 7–11.30pm, Thurs 12.30–3.30pm & 7pm–midnight, Fri 12.30–4pm & 7pm–midnight.
Dubai's only revolving restaurant, offering superlative city views.

Food is buffet only (185dh at lunch; 235dh at dinner, excluding drinks), featuring a mix of Arabian, Mediterranean and Japanese cuisines – not the city's greatest culinary experience, but a decent accompaniment to the head-turning vistas outside.

Shabestan

MAP P.36, POCKET MAP O13
Radisson Blu Dubai Deira Creek Hotel, Baniyas Rd. Union metro ☏ 04 205 7033. Daily 12.30–3pm & 7–11pm (last orders).
This posh but rather plain Iranian restaurant retains a loyal following among Emiratis and expat Iranians thanks to its huge *chelo* kebabs, fish stews and other Persian specialities like *baghalah polo* (slow-cooked lamb) and *zereshk polo* (baked chicken with wild berries). Mains 105–185dh.

Table 9

MAP P.36, POCKET MAP N4
Hilton Dubai Creek Hotel, Baniyas Rd. Al Rigga metro ☏ 04 212 7551, ⓦ facebook. com/table9dubai. Daily 6.30–11pm.

Top-notch modern European fine dining by head chef Darren Velvick and team, with an inventive and beautifully prepared selection of seasonally changing dishes. Remarkably inexpensive given the quality, especially if you opt for the three-course set menu (just 160dh including a glass of wine). Mains 75–100dh.

Vivaldi by Alfredo Russo

MAP P.36, POCKET MAP N3
Sheraton Dubai Creek Hotel, Baniyas Rd. Union metro ⓣ 04 207 1717, ⓦ vivaldidubai.com. Fri 2–4pm & 7–11pm, Sat–Thurs noon–3am & 7–11pm.
Long-running Italian now sporting stylish modern decor to go with its sweeping Creek views. The menu (by Michelin-starred Alfredo Russo) features artful modern Italian mains (120–140dh) alongside a good and reasonably priced selection of pasta and pizza (from 60dh), and there's a DJ Tues–Thurs from 8pm and Fri 2–4pm.

Bars

Issimo Bar

MAP P.36, POCKET MAP N4
Hilton Dubai Creek Hotel, Baniyas Rd. Al Rigga metro ⓣ 04 227 1111. Daily 3pm–1am.
Chic little cocktail joint with a cute boat-shaped bar and a refreshingly unposey atmosphere – and also one of the city's few nonsmoking drinking holes. A good spot for an aperitif or digestif before or after a meal at *Table 9* (see opposite) upstairs.

The Pub

MAP P.36, POCKET MAP O13
Radisson Blu Dubai Deira Creek Hotel, Baniyas Rd. Union metro ⓣ 04 222 7171. Daily noon–1pm & 6pm–2am.
Spacious and usually fairly peaceful English-style pub, complete with the usual fake wooden bar and lots of TVs screening global sports.

Happy hour (20 percent discounts) daily 6–9pm.

Up on the Tenth

MAP P.36, POCKET MAP O13
10th floor, Radisson Blu Dubai Deira Creek Hotel, Baniyas Rd. Union metro ⓣ 04 222 7171. Daily 6.30pm–3am.
One of Dubai's best-kept secrets, offering just about the best Creek views to be had in the city centre. Arrive early, grab a window seat and watch the city light up. A jazz singer and pianist perform nightly (except Tues) from 10pm.

Shisha

Creek View Restaurant

MAP P.36, POCKET MAP O13
Baniyas Rd. Baniyas Square metro ⓣ 04 223 3223. Daily 10am–2am.
This convivial open-air café scores highly for its breezy creekside location and lively late-night atmosphere. It's a good place for an after-dinner smoke (with thirteen types of shisha at 18–30dh) and coffee, although the food (mainly mezze and kebabs) is mediocre and best avoided. No alcohol.

Issimo Bar

The inner suburbs

Fringing the southern and eastern edges of the city centre – and separating it from the more modern areas beyond – is a necklace of low-key suburbs: Garhoud, Oud Metha, Karama and Satwa. South of Deira, workaday Garhoud is home to the Dubai Creek Golf Club, with its famously futuristic clubhouse, and the adjacent yacht club, where you'll find a string of attractive waterside restaurants alongside the lovely *Park Hyatt* hotel. Directly over the Creek, Oud Metha is home to the quirky Wafi complex and the lavish Khan Murjan Souk, while west of here the enjoyably downmarket suburbs of Karama and Satwa are both interesting places to get off the tourist trail and see something of local life among the city's Indian and Filipino expats, with plenty of cheap curry houses and shops selling designer fakes.

Garhoud

MAP P.44, POCKET MAP N5–07
Deira City Centre metro.

Covering the area between the airport and the Creek, the suburb of **Garhoud** is an interesting mishmash of up- and downmarket attractions. The **Deira City Centre** mall (see page 47) is the main draw for locals, while on the far side of Baniyas Road lies the **Dubai Creek Golf Club**, an impressive swathe of lush fairways centred on the quirky clubhouse, with its uniquely spiky white roofline echoing the shape of a dhow's sails and masts. Close by you'll find the **Dubai Creek Yacht Club**, occupying a full-sized replica of a ship's bridge, with dozens of beautiful yachts moored alongside and a cluster of good restaurants lining the waterfront. Next door sits the beguiling **Park Hyatt** hotel, its serene white Moroccan-style buildings, topped with vivid blue-tiled domes, adding a further touch of style to the creekside hereabouts.

Wafi

MAP P.44, POCKET MAP L6

Junction of Oud Metha and Sheikh Rashid roads. Dubai Healthcare City metro ☏ 04 324 4555, ⓦ wafi.com. Daily 10am–10pm (Thurs & Fri until midnight).

The wacky Egyptian-themed **Wafi** complex is a little slice of Vegas in Dubai, dotted with obelisks, pharaonic statues, random hieroglyphs and assorted miniature pyramids. The mall is home to myriad boutiques and restaurants (see pages 47 and 48). The Egyptian theme is continued in the opulent **Raffles** hotel next door, built in the form of a vast pyramid, its summit capped with glass – particularly spectacular when lit up after dark.

Khan Murjan Souk

MAP P.44, POCKET MAP L6
Wafi, junction of Oud Metha and Sheikh Rashid roads. Dubai Healthcare City metro ☏ 04 324 4555, ⓦ wafi.com/souk. Daily 10am–10pm (Thurs & Fri until midnight).

Hidden away between Wafi and the *Raffles* hotel, **Khan Murjan Souk** is one of Dubai's finest "traditional" developments, allegedly modelled after the fabled fourteenth-century Khan Murjan Souk in Baghdad.

Shopping for fakes

Despite occasional government clampdowns, Dubai's vibrant trade in **counterfeit goods** (bags, watches, sunglasses, pens, DVDs and so on) is still going strong. Spend any amount of time in Karama Souk, the Gold Souk or around Al Fahidi Street in Bur Dubai and you'll be repeatedly importuned with offers of "cheap copy watches" or "copy bags", as the souks' enthusiastic touts euphemistically describe them. Many fakes are still relatively expensive – you're unlikely to find bigger-ticket items for much under US$50, and plenty of items cost double that, although they'll still be a lot cheaper than the real thing. Fakes may look convincing but longevity varies considerably; some items can fall to pieces within a fortnight, and it's essential to check quality carefully – particularly stitching and zips – and be prepared to shop around and bargain like crazy.

The souk is divided into four sections – Egyptian, Syrian, Moroccan and Turkish (not that you can really tell the difference) – spread over two underground levels, with a lovely outdoor restaurant at its centre (see page 48) and some 125 shops selling all manner of traditional wares. It's a great (albeit pricey) place to shop, while the faux-Arabian decor is impressively done, with lavish detailing ranging from intricately carved wooden balconies to enormous Moroccan lanterns and colourful tilework.

Creek Park

MAP P.44, POCKET MAP M5–7
Riyadh Rd, between Garhoud and Maktoum bridges. Dubai Healthcare City or Oud Metha metros. Daily 8am–11pm. 5dh.
Flanking the Creek, the expansive **Creek Park** serves as one of congested central Dubai's major lungs and is a pleasant place for

Wafi

THE INNER SUBURBS

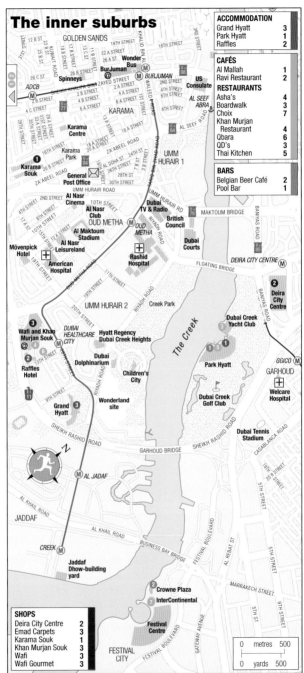

The inner suburbs

ACCOMMODATION
Grand Hyatt	3
Park Hyatt	1
Raffles	2

CAFÉS
Al Mallah	1
Ravi Restaurant	2

RESTAURANTS
Asha's	4
Boardwalk	3
Choix	7
Khan Murjan Restaurant	4
Qbara	6
QD's	3
Thai Kitchen	5

BARS
Belgian Beer Café	2
Pool Bar	1

SHOPS
Deira City Centre	2
Emad Carpets	3
Karama Souk	1
Khan Murjan Souk	3
Wafi	3
Wafi Gourmet	3

an idle ramble, with good views over the Creek towards the golf and yacht clubs. The park is nicest towards dusk, when the temperature falls and the place fills up a bit, although it can be eerily deserted during weekdays. It's particularly good for kids, with plenty of playgrounds and the fun **Children's City** (see page 117) to explore, as well as the **Dubai Dolphinarium** (see page 117). Children (and, indeed, adults) may also be tempted by the park's **cable car**, which offers half-hour trips (25dh; children 10dh) dangling 30m up in the air.

Karama

MAP P.44, POCKET MAP L3–4
Karama metro.

Karama is the classic Dubai inner-city suburb, home to some of the legions of Indian, Pakistani and Filipino expat workers who supply so much of the city's labour. The district is centred on **Kuwait Street** and the bustling little **Karama Centre**, with colourful shops selling *shalwar kameez* and Indian-style jewellery. At the end of Kuwait Street lies the lively **Karama Park**, surrounded by cheap and cheery Indian restaurants. South of here is the district's main tourist attraction, the **Karama Souk**, with hundreds of small shops stuffed full of fake designer clothes, watches, glasses, DVDs and other items.

Satwa

POCKET MAP H2–J2

The unpretentious district of **Satwa** is the most southerly of Dubai's predominantly low-rise, low-income inner suburbs before you reach the giant skyscrapers of Sheikh Zayed Road. It's also one of the few places in Dubai where the city's different ethnic groups really rub shoulders, reflected in an unusually eclectic selection of places to eat, from cheap-and-cheerful curry houses to Lebanese shwarma cafés and Western fast-food joints.

At the centre of the district lies **Satwa Roundabout**. The streets south of here are mainly occupied by Indian and Pakistani shops and cafés, including the well-known *Ravi's* (see page 47). West from the roundabout stretches the tree-lined **2 December Street** (formerly Al Diyafah Street), one of the nicest in Dubai – and one of the few outside the city centre boasting any real street life – with dozens of restaurants and an interestingly cosmopolitan atmosphere.

Festival City

MAP P.44, POCKET MAP M9
Festival Boulevard ⓦ dubaifestivalcity. com.

Festival City is one of Dubai's newest and largest purpose-built neighbourhoods – a self-contained city within a city, complete with villas and apartments, offices, golf course, marina, shopping mall and a pair of swanky five-star hotels. The centrepiece of the development is the bright, modern **Festival Centre** shopping mall: relatively small beer compared to other malls around the city, although there are fine, sweeping views from the

Satwa

Karama Souk

waterfront promenade outside across the water to the dhow-building yards at Jaddaf and the long line of skyscrapers beyond.

Ras al Khor Wildlife Sanctuary

POCKET MAP Q8

Ras al Khor/Oud Metha roads ☏ 04 606 6831 or ☏ 04 606 6826, Ⓦ bit.ly/rasalkhor. Oct–March: daily 7.30am–5.30pm, Fri 2–5.30pm; April–Sept: daily 6am–6pm, Fri 2–6pm. Free.

Some 8km inland, the Dubai Creek widens into the impressive **Ras al Khor** ("Head of the Creek"), forming an extensive inland lagoon dotted with mangroves and surrounded by intertidal salt and mud flats – a unique area of unspoilt nature close to the city centre. The southern end of the lagoon is home to the low-key **Ras al Khor Wildlife Sanctuary**, best known for its aquatic birdlife. The sanctuary is an important stopover on winter migratory routes from East Africa to West Asia and almost seventy different species have been spotted here. It's best known for the colourful flocks of bright pink flamingoes which nest here – one of Dubai's most surreal sights when seen perched against the smoggy outlines of the city skyscrapers beyond. You can't actually go into the sanctuary, but you can birdwatch from one of two **hides** on its edge. Signage for the hides is minimal and you'll need a car to reach them, but don't expect taxi drivers to know where they are.

Meydan

INSIDE FRONT COVER FLAP

Meydan Rd (take exit 7 off the E66 Al Ain Rd, or exit 20 off Al Khail Rd (E44), around 4km south of Ras al Khor Ⓦ meydan.ae.

The vast **Meydan** complex provides conclusive proof of the ruling Maktoum family's passion – bordering on obsession – for all things equine. Founder of Godolphin, one of the world's most successful racing stables, Sheikh Mohammed's love of horses runs deep: he is said as a youth to have been able to tame wild horses considered unrideable by others. Centrepiece of the complex is the superb **racecourse**, opened in 2010 to provide a fitting venue for the **Dubai World Cup**, the world's richest horse race with a massive US$10 million in prize money.

Shops

Deira City Centre

MAP P.44, POCKET MAP O5
Garhoud. Deira City Centre metro
Ⓦ deiracitycentre.com. Daily 10am–10pm
(Thurs–Sat until midnight).

This big old mall remains one of
the most popular in the city, with
340-plus outlets covering the whole
retail spectrum, including oodles
of cut-price electronics alongside
fashion, jewellery and perfumes
in all price ranges. Ali Al Jazeeri
(on the top floor) is a great place
to pick up a set of haute-couture
Emirati-style robes plus headdress.

Emad Carpets

MAP P.44, POCKET MAP L6
Wafi, Oud Metha. Dubai Healthcare City
metro Ⓣ 04 324 2206. Daily 8.30am–
midnight.

Home branch of the city's
leading chain of superior carpet
sellers, with gorgeous (and, not
surprisingly, pricey) rugs from
Iran, Turkey, Afghanistan, Central
Asia and Pakistan, plus kilims and
pashminas. Also has branches in
the Dubai Mall and Souk al Bahar.

Karama Souk

MAP P.44, POCKET MAP L4
Karama. ADCB metro. Most shops open
daily 10am–10pm.

The best place to find fake designer
gear, with dozens of shops stacked
full of imitation designer clothing
and bags and "genuine fake
watches". There are also a few low-
grade souvenir shops dotted around
the souk selling kitsch classics like
miniature Burj al Arabs moulded
in glass.

Khan Murjan Souk

MAP P.44, POCKET MAP L6
Wafi, Oud Metha. Dubai Healthcare City
metro Ⓦ wafi.com/souk-in-dubai. Daily
10am–10pm (Thurs & Fri until midnight).

The hundred-plus stores in this
superb replica souk (see page 42)
comprise the city's best and most
upmarket array of traditional crafts
shops, selling just about every kind
of Arabian gewgaw, artefact and
antique you can think of.

Wafi

MAP P.44, POCKET MAP L6
Oud Metha. Dubai Healthcare City metro
Ⓦ wafi.com. Daily 10am–10pm (Thurs &
Fri until midnight).

This zany Egyptian-themed mall
makes for a pleasantly superior
shopping experience, with branches
of Wafi Gourmet (see below),
Emad Carpets (see opposite) and
some good fashion boutiques,
including local ladieswear favourite
Ginger & Lace.

Wafi Gourmet

MAP P.44, POCKET MAP L6
Wafi, Oud Metha. Dubai Healthcare City
metro Ⓣ 04 327 9940, Ⓦ wafigourmet.
com. Daily 10am–10pm (Thurs & Fri until
midnight).

The ultimate Dubai deli, piled high
with tempting Middle Eastern
items, including big buckets of
olives, nuts, spices and dried fruits,
and trays of date rolls, baklava and
fine chocolates, plus an attached
café. Also has branches in Dubai
Mall and Festival City.

Cafés

Al Mallah

POCKET MAP J2
Al Diyafah St. Al Jafiliya metro Ⓣ 600 522
521. Daily 7am–11am.

A classic slice of Satwa nightlife,
this no-frills Lebanese café churns
out good shwarmas, grills and other
Middle Eastern food at bargain
prices (mezze 12–20dh, mains
30–60dh) to a lively local crowd;
the pavement terrace is a great
place to people-watch.

Ravi Restaurant

POCKET MAP J2
Satwa Rd, just south of Satwa Roundabout.
Al Jafiliya metro. Ⓣ 04 331 5353. Daily
5am–3am.

This famous little Pakistani café, located between the copycat *Ravi Palace* and *Rawi Palace* restaurants, attracts a loyal local and expat clientele thanks to its tasty and inexpensive array of subcontinental standards (mains 16–25dh). There's seating inside, but it's more fun (despite the traffic) to sit out on the pavement and watch the street life of Satwa drift by.

Restaurants

Asha's

MAP P.44, POCKET MAP L6

Wafi, Oud Metha. Dubai Healthcare City metro ☎ 04 324 4100, ⓦ ashasrestaurants. com. Daily 12.30–3.30pm & 7pm–midnight.

Named after legendary Bolly-wood chanteuse Asha Bhosle, with sleek modern orange decor and an interesting menu featuring traditional North Indian classics alongside recipes from Bhosle's own family cookbook. Mains 60–175dh.

Boardwalk

MAP P.44, POCKET MAP N6

Dubai Creek Yacht Club, Garhoud. Deira City

Boardwalk

Centre metro ☎ 04 295 6000, ⓦ dubaigolf. com/dubai-creek-golf-yacht-club. Sun–Thurs noon–midnight, Fri & Sat 8am–midnight.

Sleek, recently refurbished restaurant on the yacht club's creekside boardwalk, with stunning city views and a mainly Italian and Mediterranean-style menu featuring lots of seafood and pizza, plus tasty antipasti.

Choix

MAP P.44, POCKET MAP N6

InterContinental Hotel, Dubai Festival City. ☎ 04 701 01111, ⓦ dubaifestivalcityhotels. com/choix. Daily 7am–9.30pm.

New restaurant by three Michelin-star French chef Pierre Gagnaire, serving similar cuisine to his previous Parisian restaurant, Reflects – with the addition of a patisserie where you can enjoy a great morning coffee and fresh baguette. Popular for business meetings, which was probably the whole idea.

Khan Murjan Restaurant

MAP P.44, POCKET MAP L6

Souk Khan Murjan, Wafi, Oud Metha. Dubai Healthcare City metro ☎ 04 327 9795. Daily 10am–2am. The centrepiece of the spectacular Souk Khan Murjan, this beautiful courtyard restaurant has proved a big hit with the city's Emiratis and expat Arabs, thanks to the traditional atmosphere and unusually wide-ranging menu, featuring tempting selections from assorted Middle Eastern cuisines. Mains 75–85dh.

Qbara

MAP P.44. POCKET MAP L6

Al Razi St (next to Raffles hotel). Dubai Healthcare City metro ☎ 04 709 2500, ⓦ qbara.ae. Daily 6pm–1am.

Gorgeously romantic restaurant-cum-lounge-bar – it feels like being inside a rather sexy planetarium. Food is fine-dining with a pronounced Arabian twist, featuring inventive and mouthwatering mezze and mains

Ravi Restaurant

(100–170dh), plus grills and Australian steaks.

QD's

MAP P.44, POCKET MAP N6
Dubai Creek Yacht Club, Garhoud. Deira City Centre metro ☎ 04 295 6000, Ⓦ dubaigolf. com/dubai-creek-golf-yacht-club. Daily 5pm–2am, Thurs, Fri & Sat till 3am.
Fun and good-value restaurant, bar and shisha café in a superb location on a large open-air terrace overlooking the Creek. The cheap and cheerful pub-grub-style menu features lots of pizzas and Lebanese kebabs (mains from around 50dh), and there's also a big selection of shisha and a well-stocked bar.

Thai Kitchen

MAP P.44, POCKET MAP N6
Park Hyatt Hotel, Garhoud. Deira City Centre metro ☎ 04 602 1818. Daily 7.30pm–midnight, plus Fri brunch noon–4pm.
Occupying part of the *Park Hyatt*'s lovely creekside terrace, this very smooth restaurant serves up a good range of classic Thai dishes, well prepared and with plenty of flavour and spice. Food is served in small, tapas-sized portions (42–70dh), meaning that you can sample a wide range of dishes and flavours.

Bars

Belgian Beer Café

MAP P.44, POCKET MAP M9
Crowne Plaza Hotel, Festival City
☎ 04 701 1127, Ⓦ facebook.com/ belgianbeercafedubai. Daily noon–2am (Fri & Sat until 3am).
Convivial Belgian-style pub-cum-restaurant, with an eye-catching traditional wooden interior, an excellent range of speciality beers on tap or by the bottle (including draught Hoegaarden, Leffe and Belle-Vue Kriek) and good traditional Flemish cooking.

Pool Bar

MAP P.44, POCKET MAP N6
Sheikh Rashid Rd, Park Hyatt Dubai ☎ 04 602 1814, Ⓦ tinyurl.com/PoolBarHyatt. Daily 9am–8pm.
Order your drinks while you cool off in the pool at this swim-up bar. Also serves finger food and snacks, nothing that would make you stay out of the water for too long.

Sheikh Zayed Road and Downtown Dubai

Around 5km south of the Creek, the upwardly mobile suburbs of southern Dubai begin in spectacular style with the massed skyscrapers of Sheikh Zayed Road and the huge Downtown Dubai development: an extraordinary sequence of neck-cricking high-rises which march south from the landmark Emirates Towers to the cloud-capped Burj Khalifa, the world's tallest building. This is the modern city at its most futuristic and flamboyant, and perhaps the defining example of Dubai's insatiable desire to offer more luxury, more glitz and more retail opportunities than the competition, with a string of record-breaking attractions which now include not just the world's tallest building but also its largest mall, tallest hotel and biggest fountain.

Emirates Towers

MAP P.52, POCKET MAP G4
Sheikh Zayed Rd. Emirates Towers metro
Ⓦ bit.ly/JEThotel.

Opened in 2000, the soaring **Emirates Towers** remain one of modern Dubai's most iconic

Emirates Towers

symbols, despite increasing competition from newer and even more massive landmarks. The larger office tower (355m) was the tallest building in the Middle East and tenth highest in the world when it was completed, though now it barely scrapes into the top ten tallest buildings in the city.

The taller tower houses the offices of Emirates airlines; the smaller is occupied by the exclusive *Jumeirah Emirates Towers* hotel (see page 101). The office tower isn't open to the public, but there are plenty of opportunities to look around the hotel tower, most spectacularly from the 51st-floor *Alta Badia* bar (see page 58).

Dubai International Financial Centre

MAP P.52, POCKET MAP G4
Between Sheikh Zayed Rd and 312 Rd.
Emirates Tower metro Ⓦ difc.ae.

The **Dubai International Financial Centre (DIFC)** is the city's financial hub and home to myriad banks, investment companies and other enterprises. The DIFC's northern end is marked by **The Gate**, a striking building looking like a kind of postmodern Arc de Triomphe-cum-office block. The Gate is surrounded on three sides by further buildings linked by "The Balcony", an attractive raised terrace lined with assorted cafés and shops. Off on the east side of the complex is the **Gate Village**, now one of the focal points of Dubai's burgeoning visual arts scene, with virtually every building occupied by assorted galleries.

Dubai World Trade Centre

MAP P.52, POCKET MAP J4
Sheikh Zayed Rd, by Trade Centre
Roundabout. World Trade Centre metro
Ⓦ dwtc.com.

On the north side of the sprawling **Dubai International Convention and Exhibition Centre** rises the venerable old **Dubai World Trade Centre** tower, Dubai's first skyscraper. Commissioned in 1979 by the visionary Sheikh Rashid, then ruler of Dubai, this 39-storey edifice was widely regarded as a massive white elephant when it was first built, standing as it did in the middle of what was then empty desert far from the old city centre. Contrary to expectations it proved an enormous success, serving as an important anchor for future development along the strip and fully justifying Sheikh Rashid's far-sighted ambition.

Along Sheikh Zayed Road

MAP P.52, POCKET MAP F4–H4
A more or less unbroken line of high-rises lines Sheikh Zayed Road south of the Emirates Towers. Heading down the strip brings you almost immediately to the daft **Al Yaqoub Tower**: effectively a postmodern replica of London's Big Ben, although at 330m it's well over three times the height of the 96m-tall UK landmark.

Continuing down the road brings you to the graceful **Rose Rayhaan**, at 333m formerly the world's tallest hotel until the opening of the *JW Marriott Marquis Dubai* in nearby

Al Yaqoub Tower

Business Bay, while slightly further south the strip reaches a suitably dramatic end with the iconic **Dusit Thani** hotel, a towering glass-and-metal edifice inspired by the traditional Thai *wai*, a prayer-like gesture of welcome, though it looks more like a huge upended tuning fork thrust into the ground.

Burj Khalifa

MAP P.52, POCKET MAP E4
Sheikh Mohammed bin Rashid Blvd (Emaar
Blvd), Downtown Dubai. Burj Khalifa/Dubai
Mall metro Ⓣ 04 888 8888, Ⓦ burjkhalifa.
ae. At the Top tours depart from the ticket
desk in the lower-ground floor of the Dubai
Mall (daily 8.30am–6pm). Prices vary
according to the time of day, rising during
late-afternoon/sunset "prime hours" and
costing 125–200dh if prebooked online,
or 300dh for immediate admission. At
the Top Sky Experience tickets (must be
prebooked) cost 300/500dh.

Rising imperiously skywards at the southern end of Sheikh Zayed Road stands the needle-thin **Burj Khalifa**, the world's tallest building. Opened in early 2010 after five years' intensive construction, the Burj finally topped out at a

52

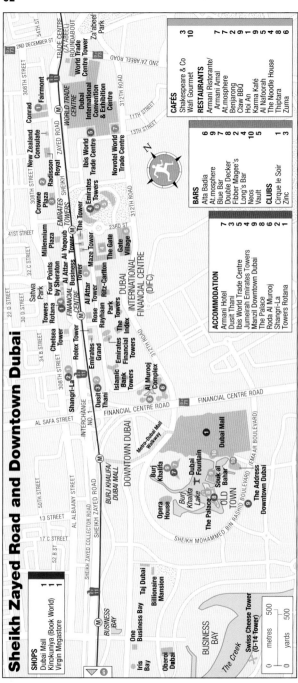

Sheikh Zayed Road and Downtown Dubai

SHOPS
Dubai Mall	1
Kinokuniya (Book World)	1
Virgin Megastore	1

ACCOMMODATION
Armani Hotel	7
Dusit Thani	3
Ibis World Trade Centre	5
Jumeirah Emirates Towers	4
Manzil Downtown Dubai	9
The Palace	8
Roda Al Murooj	10
Shangri-La	2
Towers Rotana	1

BARS
Alta Badia	7
At.mosphere	3
Blue Bar	5
Double Decker	4
Fibber Magee's	9
Long's Bar	8
Neos	6
Vault	2

CLUBS
Cirque le Soir	1
Zinc	3

CAFÉS
Shakespeare & Co	3
Wafi Gourmet	10

RESTAURANTS
Armani Ristorante/	7
Armani Amal	7
At.mosphere	3
Benjarong	9
Claw BBQ	1
Hoi An	9
Karma Kafé	5
Al Natoorah	4
The Noodle House	8
Thiptara	8
Zuma	6

staggering 828m, comprehensively smashing all existing world records. The astonishing scale of the Burj is difficult to fully comprehend – the building is best appreciated at a distance, from where you can properly appreciate its jaw-dropping height.

Access to the Burj Khalifa is strictly controlled. Most visitors opt for a visit to the "At the Top" observation deck on floor 124, offering sensational views; alternatively, the seriously pricey "At the Top Sky Experience" gives you access to floor 124 along with a second, even loftier observation deck on floor 148, although the slight gain in height doesn't really justify the hefty ticket price. The tour also includes some interesting displays on the creation of the tower.

Dubai Mall

MAP P.52, POCKET MAP E5–F5
Financial Centre Rd. Burj Khalifa/Dubai Mall metro ⓦ thedubaimall.com. Daily 10am–midnight.

Right next to the Burj Khalifa is the supersized **Dubai Mall**, with over 1200 shops spread across four floors and covering over a million square

metres – making it easily the largest mall in the world measured by total area. Attractions here include the Dubai Aquarium (see below), Kidzania (see page 117) and an Olympic-sized ice rink; The Souk provides an incongruous home for the "Dubai Dino", the beautifully preserved skeleton of a 150-million-year-old *Diplodocus longus*. Look out too for the eye-catching **The Waterfall**, complete with life-sized statues of fibreglass divers.

Dubai Aquarium and Underwater Zoo

MAP P.52, POCKET MAP F5
Dubai Mall. Burj Khalifa/Dubai Mall metro ⓣ 04 448 5200, ⓦ thedubaiaquarium. com. Daily 10am–midnight, last admission 11.30pm. From 130dh.

Assuming you enter the Dubai Mall's main entrance off Financial Centre Road, one of the first things you'll see is the spectacular viewing panel of the **Dubai Aquarium and Underwater Zoo**: a huge, transparent floor-to-ceiling aquarium filled to the brim with fish big and small, including some large and spectacularly ugly grouper.

Dubai Fountain

Dubai Fountain

MAP P.52, POCKET MAP E5
Burj Khalifa Lake, Downtown Dubai. Burj
Khalifa/Dubai Mall metro ☎ 04 362 7500,
ⓦ bit.ly/TheDubaiFountain. Displays daily
every 30min 6–11pm, plus 1pm & 1.30pm
except Fri.

Winding through the heart of
Downtown Dubai is the large
Burj Khalifa Lake, a section of
which doubles as the spectacular
275m-long **Dubai Fountain**, the
world's biggest, capable of shooting
jets of water up to 150m high,
and illuminated with over 6000
lights and 25 colour projectors.
The fountain really comes to life
after dark, spouting carefully
choreographed watery flourishes
which "dance" elegantly in time
to a range of Arabic, Hindi and
classical songs, viewable from
anywhere around the lake for free.
Short (25min) **abra** rides around
the lake/fountain are also available
(daily 5.45–11.30pm; 65dh),
leaving from outside *Wafi Gourmet*
in the lake-facing side of the Dubai
Mall.

Old Town

MAP P.52, POCKET MAP E5
Burj Khalifa/Dubai Mall metro. Souk Al
Bahar. Sat–Thurs 10am–10pm, Fri 2–10pm.
The chintzy **Old Town** development
comprises a low-rise sprawl of sand-
coloured buildings with traditional
Moorish styling. Centrepiece is the
Souk al Bahar, a small, Arabian-
themed mall, pleasantly peaceful
after neighbouring Dubai Mall.
A string of restaurants lines the
waterfront terrace outside, offering
peerless views of Burj Khalifa.

Business Bay

MAP P.52, POCKET MAP C4–D5
Business Bay metro.
Dubai's last big hurrah before the
credit crunch hit town in 2008, the
vast **Business Bay** development
comprises a dense cluster of high-
rises arranged around an extension
of the Creek. Most of the buildings
are fairly humdrum, although there
are a few local landmarks worth
a quick look. Close to the metro,
the **JW Marriott Marquis Dubai**
is currently the tallest hotel in
the world at a cool 355m, while
opposite the *Marriott* stands the
extraordinary crescent-shaped **Iris
Bay** building. Further down the
road, you can't fail to notice the
funky O-14 building, popularly
known as the **Swiss Cheese Tower**
thanks to the undulating layer of
white cladding that envelops the
entire structure, dotted with around
1300 circular holes and looking
uncannily like an enormous piece of
postmodern Emmenthal cheese.

Souk al Bahar

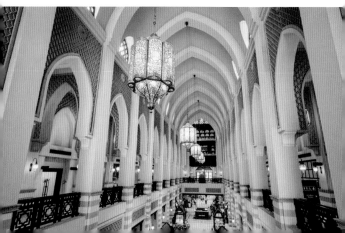

Shops

Dubai Mall

MAP P.52, POCKET MAP E5–F5
Downtown Dubai. Burj Khalifa/Dubai Mall
metro Ⓦ thedubaimall.com. Daily 10am–
midnight.

Highlights in this mother of
all malls include the flagship
Bloomingdale's and Galeries
Lafayette department stores;
"Fashion Avenue", home to the
biggest array of designer labels
in Dubai; and the attractively
chintzy "Souk" area, with
a further 120 shops selling
gold, jewellery and Arabian
perfumes. Upstairs you'll find a
Dubai branch of Hamleys, the
famous London toyshop; Não
do Brasil, an eye-catching shop
stuffed full of funky trainers;
and Kinokuniya and Virgin
(see below).

Kinokuniya (Book World)

MAP P.52, POCKET MAP E5
Second floor, Dubai Mall. Burj Khalifa/
Dubai Mall metro Ⓣ 04 434 0111, Ⓦ uae.
kinokuniya.com. Daily 10am–midnight.
This local outpost of the famous
Japanese chain is far and away
Dubai's best bookshop – a vast
emporium stuffed with a simply
massive array of titles, ranging
from mainstream novels, travel
guides and magazines through
to graphic novels and a brilliant
manga selection.

Virgin Megastore

MAP P.52, POCKET MAP E5
Dubai Mall. Burj Khalifa/Dubai Mall metro
Ⓣ 04 325 3330, Ⓦ virginmegastore.
me. Daily 10am–10pm (Thurs–Sat until
midnight).
This Dubai offshoot of the
defunct UK chain sells all sort
of electronics and gadgets but is
mainly of interest for its excellent
CD selection, with music from
across the Middle east, plus
recordings by many Gulf and
Emirati artists.

Wafi Gourmet

Cafés

Shakespeare & Co

MAP P.52, POCKET MAP G4
South side of Al Saqr Business Tower, 37th
St, off Sheikh Zayed Rd, roughly opposite
the Ritz-Carlton Hotel. Financial Centre
metro Ⓣ 04 331 1757, Ⓦ shakespeare-
and-co.com. Daily 7am–1am.
The original branch of a citywide
café chain, characterized by its
distinctively chintzy decor – a
kind of pastel-coloured high-camp
Victoriana, usually with cherubs.
Food includes a wide selection
of soups, salads, sandwiches and
crêpes (from 35dh), plus more
substantial mains.

Wafi Gourmet

MAP P.52, POCKET MAP E5
Dubai Mall. Burj Khalifa/Dubai Mall metro
Ⓣ 04 330 8297, Ⓦ wafigourmet.com. Daily
10am–2am.
A brilliant waterside location in
front of the Dubai Fountain is
the main draw at this branch of
the local deli-plus-café chain (see
page 47), although you'll have
to arrive early or get lucky to
bag one of the coveted fountain-

facing tables. Food features mouthwatering local delicacies, a great range of authentic mezze and more substantial Lebanese-style seafood and meat grills (65–90dh).

Restaurants

Armani Ristorante/ Armani Amal

MAP P.52, POCKET MAP E4
Burj Khalifa. Burj Khalifa/Dubai Mall metro ⓘ 04 888 3666, Ⓦ dubai.armanihotels.com. Daily 5–11.30pm.
There are a number of upmarket dining options tucked away inside the suave *Armani* hotel. Top billing goes to the signature *Armani Ristorante*, serving fine-dining regional Italian cuisine (mains 130–290dh), while *Armani Amal* also gets good reviews for its inventive regional Indian cuisine with a European twist (mains 120–190dh). Note that if you're not staying at the hotel you'll need an advance reservation to gain admittance.

At.mosphere

MAP P.52, POCKET MAP H3
Burj Khalifa, Downtown Dubai. Burj Khalifa/Dubai Mall metro ⓘ 04 888 3828, Ⓦ atmosphereburjkhalifa.com. Daily 7pm–midnight.
At.mosphere's selling point couldn't be simpler: this is the world's highest bar and restaurant, located almost half a kilometre above ground level on the 122nd floor of the soaring Burj Khalifa. Decor is svelte and modern, although your eyes will inevitably be drawn to the huge views outside. Choose between the chic restaurant (set lunches 450/600dh for 2/3 courses; dinner à la carte mains 200–450dh) or the more laidback lounge (80–250dh). There's a minimum per-person spend of 200–500dh for some tables with views.

Benjarong

MAP P.52, POCKET MAP F4
Dusit Thani Hotel, Sheikh Zayed Rd. Financial Centre metro ⓘ 04 343 3333. Daily noon–3.30pm & 7–11pm.
Set in a delicately painted wooden pavilion on the 24th floor of the *Dusit Thani*, *Benjarong* offers some of the best Royal Thai cooking in Dubai. There's a particularly good selection of fish and seafood, plus the usual meat stir-fries and red and yellow curries, and they also do a lively Friday brunch. Mains 75–145dh.

Hoi An

MAP P.52, POCKET MAP E5
Shangri-La hotel, Sheikh Zayed Rd. Financial Centre metro ⓘ 04 343 8888, Ⓦ shangri-la.com. Daily 7pm–midnight.
Hybrid Vietnamese–French cuisine is the speciality here, served in an elegant colonial-style restaurant. Traditional Vietnamese dishes are combined with modern cooking techniques to produce unusual creations like the signature sea bass in lotus leaf with galangal and kumquat compote. Mains 138–172dh.

Karma Kafe

MAP P.52, POCKET MAP E5
Souk al Bahar. Burj Khalifa/Dubai Mall metro ⓘ 04 423 0909, Ⓦ karma-kafe.com. Sun–Thurs 3pm–2am, Fri 1pm–2am, Sat noon–2am; drinks 3pm–2am.
Sister establishment to the ever-popular *Buddha Bar*, with a vaguely Japanese-looking interior and pleasant outdoor terrace. Food is pan-Asian, with the emphasis on Korean, Japanese and Thai dishes including plenty of *sashimi*, *nigiri*, *robata*, wagyu and stir-fries (mains 89–189dh). There's a good drinks and cocktail list, too.

Al Nafoorah

MAP P.52, POCKET MAP G4
Emirates Towers Boulevard. Emirates Towers metro ⓘ 04 432 3232. Sun–Thurs noon–3.30pm, Fri & Sat noon–4pm, daily 6–11.30pm.

One of the city's best places for Middle Eastern food, *Al Nafoorah* looks more like a slightly starchy Parisian establishment than a traditional Lebanese restaurant. What's on offer is the real deal, however, from the superb array of mezze through to the perfectly cooked selection of fish, meat grills and kebabs. Mezze from 36dh, mains from 60dh.

Claw Bbq

MAP P.52, POCKET MAP E5
Souk al Bahar. Burj Khalifa/Dubai Mall metro ⓣ 04 432 2300. Sun–Thurs noon–3am, Fri & Sat 8am–2am.

A crab shack offering seafood-oriented barbecue dishes (mainly crab claws and prawns) as well as a range of meat dishes such as ribs or classic American hamburgers. There's also a simple kids' menu with corndogs or a grilled cheese sandwich. You can also indulge your sweet tooth with their Monstrous Shakes.

The Noodle House

MAP P.52, POCKET MAP G4

The Gate building. Emirates Towers metro ⓣ 04 319 8757, ⓦ thenoodlehouse.com. Daily noon–11.30pm.

A Dubai institution, this cheapish and very cheerful noodle bar caters to an endless stream of diners who huddle up on long communal tables to refuel on excellent Chinese and Southeast Asian food. No reservations, so you might have to queue at busy times. Most mains around 50–60dh.

Thiptara

MAP P.52, POCKET MAP E5
The Palace Hotel, Old Town. Burj Khalifa/ Dubai Mall metro ⓣ 04 888 3444, ⓦ theaddress.com/en/dining/thiptara. Daily 6–11.30pm.

This beautiful Thai restaurant offers probably the best night-time view of the Burj Khalifa and Dubai Fountain. The menu is strongest on seafood, but also offers a fair spread of meat dishes (though few veg options). Most mains 120–200dh. Reservations recommended.

Zuma

MAP P.52, POCKET MAP G4

Benjarong

Gate Village, Building 6. Emirates Towers metro ☎ 04 425 5660, ⓦ zumarestaurant. com. Daily: restaurant Sun–Thurs noon–3.30pm, Sat 12.30–4pm, Sat–Wed 7pm–midnight, Thurs–Fri 7pm–1am; bar 12.30pm–1 or 2am.

Very hip Japanese bar-restaurant with a dining area (including sushi counter and *robata* grill) downstairs, and a bar-lounge above. Informal *izakaya*-style dining is the order of the day, although the food itself is top-notch. Mains 110–180dh; express lunch menu 72dh. DJs nightly from around 9pm. Reservations usually essential.

Bars

Alta Badia

MAP P.52, POCKET MAP G4
51st floor, Jumeirah Emirates Tower hotel, Sheikh Zayed Rd ☎ 04 330 0000, ⓦ jumeirahemiratestowers.com. Daily 6pm–3am; ladies' nights Thurs 6–8pm.
One of the city's oldest high-rise bars, *Alta Badia* may have been unequivocally eclipsed by newer, fancier and even higher venues but remains a pleasant place for a quiet drink – and the views

Blue Bar

are still impressive. There's also a good selection of cocktails and wines on the long, Italian-inspired drinks list – excellent value during the daily 6–9pm happy hour. Women get unlimited rosé on Thursday nights.

At.mosphere

MAP P.52, POCKET MAP E4
Burj Khalifa ☎ 04 888 3828, ⓦ atmosphereburjkhalifa.com. Bar daily noon–2am.
Set on the 122nd floor of the world's tallest building, this record-breaking bar-restaurant offers the ultimate high, and a drink here is a cheaper alternative to a full-blown meal (see page 56). Advance reservations are essential and there's a minimum spend of 250dh (or 200dh for a non-window table after dark), although drinks and snacks are not extravagantly priced.

Blue Bar

MAP P.52, POCKET MAP H4
Novotel, World Trade Centre. World Trade Centre metro ☎ 04 310 8150, ⓦ facebook. com/BlueBarDubai. Thurs & Fri noon–3am, Sat–Wed noon–2am.
This stylish little bar is a pleasant spot for a mellow drink earlier in the evening, with a sedate crowd and a good selection of speciality Belgian beers, plus cocktails, wines, premium whiskies and superior bar meals. Things can get lively later on in the evening from Thursday to Saturday when there's a live band playing a mix of blues, jazz, classic rock and pop (from around 9.30pm until 1am). Happy hour daily 4–7pm (buy one, get one free).

Double Decker

MAP P.52, POCKET MAP F4
Al Murooj Rotana Hotel, Financial Centre Rd. Financial Centre metro ☎ 04 321 1111, ⓦ facebook.com/DoubleDeckerMeOfficial. Daily noon–3am.
One of the liveliest pubs in town, with quirky decor themed after the

old London Routemaster buses and usually busy with a tanked-up crowd of expats and Western tourists. Live music and/or DJ most nights from around 9pm.

Fibber Magee's

MAP P.52, POCKET MAP H3
Off Sheikh Zayed Rd. Emirates Towers metro ☏ 04 332 2400, ⓦ fibbersdubai.com. Daily noon–3am.
One of the city's best-kept secrets, and probably Dubai's most impressive stab at a traditional European pub, with a spacious, very nicely done out wood-beamed interior and a good selection of draught beers including Kilkenny, Guinness, London Pride and Peroni, plus Magners cider. There's also regular live music and good, homely pub food. To reach it, go down the small side road between *Jashan* restaurant and *Zoom* (just south of the *Radisson* hotel) and it's on your left in the bottom of the *Stables* restaurant building.

Long's Bar

MAP P.52, POCKET MAP G3
Towers Rotana Hotel, Sheikh Zayed Rd. Financial Centre metro ☏ 04 312 2202, ⓦ rotanatimes.com/towersrotana/dining/104. Daily noon–3am.
Proud home to the longest bar in the Middle East, this English-style pub offers one of the strip's more convivial and downmarket drinking holes, with all the usual tipples and the ubiquitous TV sports.

Neos

MAP P.52, POCKET MAP E5
63rd floor, The Address Downtown Dubai Hotel, Sheikh Mohammed bin Rashid Blvd (Emaar Boulevard). Burj Khalifa/Dubai Mall metro ☏ 04 888 3444, ⓦ theaddress.com. Daily 5pm–2.30am.
One of the highest bars in the city, with great views over downtown Dubai and the Burj Khalifa. There's a good drinks list and above-average food, while the bar, complete with Dubai's quirkiest columns, is almost a work of art in

its own right. Closed at the time of writing after a major fire in *The Address* hotel, but should have reopened by the time you read this.

Vault

MAP P.52, POCKET MAP C4
72nd floor, JW Marriott Marquis Hotel, Business Bay. Business Bay metro ☏ 04 414 3000, ⓦ jwmarriottmarquisdubailife.com. Daily 5pm–3am.
Dubai's second-highest bar, perched at the summit of the world's tallest hotel and offering 360° views through floor-to-ceiling windows. Fancy cocktails, bespoke spirits and fat cigars come as standard, although the daily 5–7pm happy hour keeps things a little more real, while a resident DJ (Tues–Sat from 9pm) lifts the atmosphere.

Clubs

Cirque le Soir

MAP P.52, POCKET MAP H3
Fairmont Hotel, Sheikh Zayed Rd. World Trade Centre metro ☏ 056 115 4507, ⓦ cirquelesoirdubai.com/dubai. Mon, Tues, Thurs 11pm–3am, Fri 11pm–midnight.
An offshoot of the original London club, this top-end venue is half club, half music hall, with big-top-inspired decor and assorted performers including burlesque podium dancers, kooky clowns and juggling waiters.

Zinc

MAP P.52, POCKET MAP G3
Crowne Plaza Hotel, Sheikh Zayed Rd. Emirates Towers metro ☏ 800 276 963, ⓦ facebook.com/zincnightclub. Daily 10pm–3am.
One of the longest-running and most enduringly popular clubs in Dubai, thanks to an eclectic soundtrack and unposey atmosphere. Music features a mix of retro, r'n'b, hip-hop and house, depending on the night and entrance charges (usually 50–100dh) sometimes apply, especially to men.

Jumeirah

A couple of kilometres south of the Creek, the beachside suburb of Jumeirah marks the beginning of southern Dubai's endless suburban sprawl, with swathes of chintzy low-rise villas providing a home to many of the city's European expats and other upper-income residents. The suburb is strung out along the Jumeirah Road, which arrows straight down the coast and provides the area with its principal focus, lined with a long string of shopping malls; most are fairly low-key, apart from the quirky, Italian-themed Mercato. Other attractions include the traditional Jumeirah Mosque (the only one in Dubai currently accessible to non-Muslims) and the Majlis Ghorfat um al Sheif, the former summer retreat of Dubai's erstwhile ruler Sheikh Rashid.

Jumeirah Mosque

MAP P.61, POCKET MAP H1
Jumeirah Rd. Bus #8 or #C10 ⓣ 04 353 6666, ⓦ jumeirahmosque.ae. 1hr tours Sat–Thurs at 10am. 10dh (under-5s not allowed; no pre-booking required). Public visits at 10am and 2pm (except Fridays), registration 30min before entry.

Rising proudly above the northern end of the Jumeirah Road, the stately **Jumeirah Mosque** is one of the largest and most attractive in the city, built in quasi-Fatimid (Egyptian) style, with a pair of soaring minarets, a roofline embellished with delicately carved miniature domes and richly decorated windows set in elaborate rectangular recesses. As with many of Dubai's more venerable-looking buildings though, medieval appearances are deceptive – the mosque was actually built in 1979.

It also has the added attraction of being the only mosque in Dubai that non-Muslims can visit, thanks to the regular **tours** run by the Sheikh Mohammed Centre for Cultural Understanding (see page 27). These offer a good opportunity to get a look at the mosque's rather florid interior, with its distinctive green-and-orange colour scheme and delicately painted arches, although the real draw is the informative guides, who explain some of the basic precepts and practices of Islam before inviting questions.

Mercato

MAP P.61, POCKET MAP E1
Jumeirah Rd. Bus #8 or #C10
ⓦ mercatoshoppingmall.com. Daily 10am–10pm (Thurs–Sat until midnight).

About halfway down Jumeirah Road, the eye-popping **Mercato** mall looks like a kind of miniature medieval Italian city rebuilt by the Disney Corporation. Brightly

Dubai Safari

When Dubai Zoo closed in 2017, its animals were moved to Dubai Safari park. The park is divided into five "villages" showcasing 2,500 animals from more than 250 species. Located out east in Al Warqu, it was closed for maintainance at the time of writing.

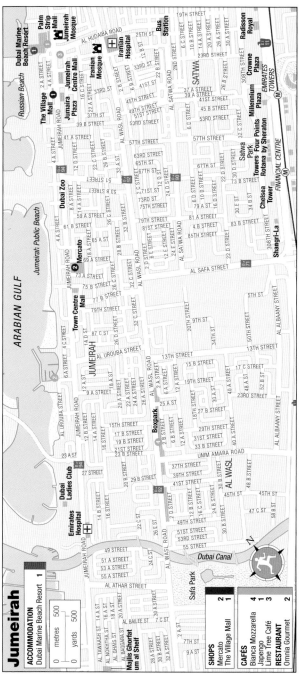

Jumeirah

ACCOMMODATION
Dubai Marine Beach Resort 1

0 metres 500
0 yards 500

SHOPS
Mercato 2
The Village Mall 1

CAFES
Bianca Mozzarella 4
Japengo 1
Lime Tree Café 3

RESTAURANT
Omnia Gourmet 2

The Dubai Canal

Unveiled in October 2013, the US$550-million **Dubai Canal** (or "Dubai Water Canal" as it's officially called) is the second and final phase in the extension of the Creek from its original terminus at Ras al Khor all the way back to the sea. The project finished in 2018, making it possible for the first time to travel between the old city, Downtown Dubai and Jumeirah by water. The canal now stretches for around 3km, with many walkways and cycle paths.

coloured quasi-Venetian-cum-Tuscan palazzi are arranged around a huge central atrium overlooked by panoramic balconies – a memorable example of the sort of brazen kitsch that Dubai does so well.

Majlis Ghorfat um al Sheif

MAP P.61, POCKET MAP A1
17 St (signed off Jumeirah Road by the BinSina pharmacy; turn down 17 St for about 50m and the majlis is on your left). Bus #8, ☏ 04226 0286. Sun–Thurs 7.30am–2.30pm. 3dh.
Tucked away just off the southern end of Jumeirah Road, the **Majlis**

Ghorfat um al Sheif offers a touching and welcome memento of old Dubai, now incongruously marooned amid an endless sea of sleek modern villas. Built in 1955 when Jumeirah was no more than a little fishing village, this modest traditional house – a simple two-storey coral-and-gypsum building embellished with fine doors and beautiful window shutters made of solid teak – was formerly used by Sheikh Rashid, the inspiration behind modern Dubai's spectacular development, as a summer house.

Majlis Ghorfat um al Sheif

Shops

Mercato

MAP P.61, POCKET MAP E1
Jumeirah Beach Rd
Ⓦ mercatoshoppingmall.com. Daily
10am–10pm (Fri until midnight).

This kitsch Italian-themed mall (see picture) packs in a good selection of rather upmarket outlets aimed at affluent local villa dwellers, including a decent range of mainstream designer labels.

The Village Mall

MAP P.61, POCKET MAP G1
Jumeirah Beach Rd. Daily 8.30am–6pm.

The best of the various small malls scattered along the northern end of Jumeirah Beach Road, home to the excellent hippy-chic S*uce, one of the city's leading independent boutiques, plus a homely little branch of *Shakespeare & Co* (see page 55).

Cafés

Bianca Mozzarella

MAP P.61, POCKET MAP D2
Boxpark, Al Wasl Rd Ⓣ 04 345 5300,
Ⓦ bianca.ae. Daily 10am–midnight.

The best of the various cafés in the quirky new Boxpark development strung out along Al Wasl Road. Super-fresh Italian food is the order of the day, served up in a sunny white dining room and featuring bright flavours and authentic ingredients (including lots of locally produced mozzarella) in its tasty selection of meat and fish mains, plus cheaper pastas and salads. Mains 50–120dh. Unlicensed.

Japengo

MAP P.61, POCKET MAP H1
Palm Strip Mall, Jumeirah Rd Ⓣ 04 345 4979. Thurs–Sat 8am–2am, Sun–Wed 7am–1am.

Bright modern café-restaurant with one of the most shamelessly eclectic menus in town, based around a

Mercato

longish list of Japanese standards (sushi, *sashimi*, *maki*) spliced together with Middle Eastern mezze, Southeast Asian stir-fries, plus pasta, sandwiches and salads. Mains 50–80dh. Branches at locations citywide, including Dubai Mall, Souk Madinat Jumeirah and Mall of the Emirates.

Lime Tree Café

MAP P.61, POCKET MAP H1
Jumeirah Rd Ⓣ 04 325 6325,
Ⓦ thelimetreecafe.com. Daily
7.30am–8pm.

Eternally popular with Jumeirah's expat wives and ladies-who-lunch, this cheery little establishment is a great place to people-watch, while food includes moreish wraps, focaccias, panini, quiches, salads and cakes, plus tasty juices.

Restaurant

Omnia Gourmet

MAP P.61, POCKET MAP D1
Jumeirah Fish Harbour 1 Shop N1–15 Ⓣ 04 343 7181, Ⓦ facebook.com/OmniaGourmet. Daily 9am–11pm.

The cool white and blue, marine-themed interior provides a pleasant, respite from the Jumeirah fishing harbour. Vegetables and fruit are organic and locally grown, and the meat is free range, even if the meals are not that varied. It's also good for a quick breakfast and offers a variety of vegetarian and vegan options.

The Burj al Arab and around

Some 18km south of the Creek, the suburb of Umm Suqeim marks the beginning of Dubai's spectacular modern beachside developments, announced with a flourish by three of Dubai's most famous landmarks: the iconic sail-shaped *Burj al Arab* hotel, the roller-coaster-like *Jumeirah Beach Hotel* and the fantastical Madinat Jumeirah complex. There are further attractions at the thrills-and-spills Wild Wadi water park and at Ski Dubai, the Middle East's first ski slope, while more sedentary pleasures can be found at the vast Mall of the Emirates, next to Ski Dubai, whose snowy pistes deliver superbly surreal views. Close to the Mall of the Emirates on the far side of Sheikh Zayed Road, the industrial area of Al Quoz provides an unlikely home to a number of Dubai's leading art galleries.

The Burj al Arab

MAP P.66, POCKET MAP K15
Off Jumeirah Rd, Umm Suqeim ⓦ burj-al-arab.com.

Rising majestically from its own man-made island just off the coast of Umm Suqeim is the peerless **Burj al Arab** ("Tower of the Arabs"). Commissioned by Dubai's ruler, Sheikh Mohammed, the aim of the Burj was simple: to serve as a global icon which would put Dubai on the international map. Money was no object. The total cost of the hotel was perhaps as much as US$2 billion, and it's been estimated that

Burj al Arab interior

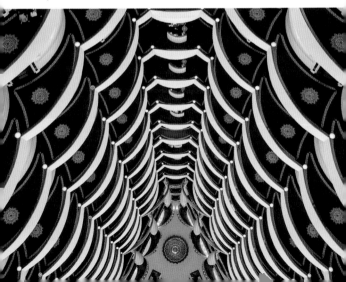

Visiting the Burj al Arab

Non-guests are only allowed into the *Burj* with a prior **reservation** at one of the hotel's bars, cafés or restaurants; call ☏ 04 301 7600 or email ✉ restaurants@jumeirah.com. Big spenders might enjoy the hotel's two fine-dining restaurants: **Al Mahara** seafood restaurant and **Al Muntaha**, at the very top of the building. The cheapest and in many ways most enjoyable option, however, is to try one of the *Burj*'s sumptuous afternoon teas (or just come for a drink) at either the **Sahn Eddar** lounge (minimum spend 290dh; afternoon teas 400/560dh) or the **Skyview Bar**, at the top of the hotel (minimum spend 350dh; afternoon tea 620dh).

even if every room in it remains full for the next hundred years, the Burj still won't pay back its original investment.

Although not much more than fifteen years old, the building's instantly recognizable outline has already established itself as a global symbol of Dubai to rival the Eiffel Tower, Big Ben and the Sydney Opera House. Even the top-floor helipad has acquired celebrity status: André Agassi and Roger Federer once famously played tennis on it, while Tiger Woods used it as a makeshift driving range, punting shots into the sea.

The Burj is home to the world's first so-called **seven-star hotel**, an expression coined by a visiting journalist to emphasize the unique levels of luxury offered within. Designed to echo the shape of a dhow's sail, the hotel's shore-facing side mainly comprises a huge sheet of white Teflon-coated fibreglass cloth, which is spectacularly illuminated by night.

Most of the **interior** is actually hollow, consisting of an enormous atrium vibrantly coloured in great swathes of red, blue and green, supported by massive, bulbous golden columns.

Staying at the *Burj al Arab* is a very expensive pleasure, and even just visiting presents certain challenges (see box). Fortunately the building's magnificent exterior can be enjoyed for free from numerous vantage points nearby.

Jumeirah Beach Hotel

MAP P.66, POCKET MAP L15
Jumeirah Rd, Umm Suqeim. Bus #8 or
#X25 ⓦ jumeirah.com.
The huge **Jumeirah Beach Hotel** (or "JBH") is the second of the area's landmark buildings, after the Burj al Arab. Designed to resemble an enormous breaking wave (although it looks more like an enormous roller coaster), and rising to a height of over 100m, the hotel was considered the most spectacular and luxurious in the city when it opened in 1997, although it has since been overtaken on both counts. It remains a fine sight, however, especially when seen from a distance in combination with the Burj al Arab, right next door, against whose slender sail it appears (with a little imagination) to be about to crash.

Wild Wadi

MAP P.66, POCKET MAP L15
Off Jumeirah Rd, Umm Suqeim. Bus #8
☏ 04 348 4444, ⓦ wildwadi.com. Daily
10am–6/7pm depending on the time of
year; ladies' nights Thurs April–Sept 8pm
to midnight. 336dh, children under 1.1m
2840dh; locker rental 48–90dh extra.
The massively popular **Wild Wadi** water park offers a variety of attractions to suit everyone from small kids to physically fit adrenaline junkies, complete with fantasy tropical lagoon, cascading waterfalls, whitewater rapids and hanging bridges. Get oriented with

a circuit of the Whitewater Wadi (Master Blaster) ride, which runs around the edge of the park, during which you're squirted on powerful jets of water up and down eleven long, twisting slides before being catapulted down the darkened Tunnel of Doom. Dedicated thrill-seekers should try the Wipeout and Riptide Flowriders, simulating powerful surfing waves, and the park's stellar attraction, the **Jumeirah Sceirah**, the world's eighth highest waterslide.

Madinat Jumeirah

MAP P.66, POCKET MAP K15–16
Al Sufouh Rd, Al Sufouh. Bus #8
Ⓦ madinatjumeirah.com.

A vast mass of faux-Moorish-style buildings, the huge **Madinat Jumeirah** complex rises high above the coastal highway. Opened in 2005, the Madinat is one of Dubai's most spectacular modern developments: a self-contained miniature "Arabian" city comprising a vast sprawl of sand-coloured buildings topped by an extraordinary quantity of wind towers, the whole thing arranged around a sequence of meandering palm-fringed waterways along which visitors are chauffeured in replica abras.

There's an undeniable whiff of Disneyland about the entire complex, admittedly, although the sheer scale of the place is strangely compelling. The Madinat also offers some of the most eye-boggling views in Dubai, with the futuristic outlines of the Burj al Arab surreally framed between medieval-looking wind towers and Moorish arcading.

The obvious place from which to explore the complex is the **Souk Madinat Jumeirah** (see page 68), though it's well worth investigating some of the superb restaurants and bars in the *Al Qasr*

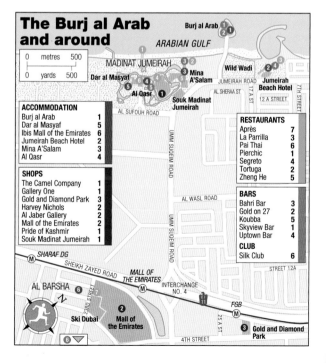

The Burj al Arab and around

| 0 | metres | 500 |
| 0 | yards | 500 |

ARABIAN GULF

Burj al Arab ❶ ❶

MADINAT JUMEIRAH

Dar al Masyaf

Al Qasr ❶

Mina A'Salam ❸

Wild Wadi ❷ ❸ ❹

Jumeirah Beach Hotel ❷

Souk Madinat Jumeirah

JUMEIRAH ROAD
AL SHERAA ST
AL SUFOUH ROAD

UMM SUQEIM ROAD

AL WASL ROAD

UMM SUQEIM ROAD

12 A STREET
17 A ST
12 A STREET
7TH STREET

ACCOMMODATION
Burj al Arab	1
Dar al Masyaf	5
Ibis Mall of the Emirates	6
Jumeirah Beach Hotel	2
Mina A'Salam	3
Al Qasr	4

SHOPS
The Camel Company	1
Gallery One	1
Gold and Diamond Park	3
Harvey Nichols	2
Al Jaber Gallery	2
Mall of the Emirates	2
Pride of Kashmir	1
Souk Madinat Jumeirah	1

RESTAURANTS
Après	7
La Parrilla	3
Pai Thai	6
Pierchic	1
Segreto	4
Tortuga	2
Zheng He	5

BARS
Bahri Bar	3
Gold on 27	2
Koubba	5
Skyview Bar	1
Uptown Bar	4

CLUB
Silk Club	6

SHARAF DG Ⓜ

SHEIKH ZAYED ROAD

MALL OF THE EMIRATES

INTERCHANGE NO. 4

AL BARSHA ❻

23RD STREET

Ski Dubai ❻

Mall of the Emirates ❷

FGB Ⓜ

STREET 12A

25.4 ST
25.5 ST

Gold and Diamond Park ❸

4TH STREET

Madinat Jumeirah

and *Mina A'Salam* hotels, several of which offer superlative views over the Madinat itself, the Burj al Arab and coastline.

Mall of the Emirates

MAP P.66, POCKET MAP J18–K18
Interchange 4, Sheikh Zayed Rd. Mall of the Emirates metro Ⓦ malloftheemirates. com. Daily 10am–10pm (Thurs–Sat until midnight).

The second-largest mall in Dubai (outdone only by the Dubai Mall), the swanky **Mall of the Emirates** is one of the most popular in the city, packed with hundreds of shops and crowds of locals and tourists alike. For dedicated shopaholics it's one of the best places in Dubai to splash some cash (see page 68) – and there's also the added bonus of surreal views of the snow-covered slopes of Ski Dubai through huge glass walls at the western end of the mall, or from one of the various restaurants and bars overlooking the slopes, such as *Après* (see page 69).

Ski Dubai

MAP P.66, POCKET MAP J18
Mall of the Emirates, Interchange 4, Sheikh Zayed Rd. Mall of the Emirates metro Ⓣ 071 800 386, Ⓦ skidxb.com. Daily 10am–11pm (Thurs–Fri until midnight). 2hr ski slope session adult 200dh, children 170dh; ski slope day-pass 305/280dh.

Attached to the Mall of the Emirates, the huge **Ski Dubai** is unquestionably one of the city's weirder ideas: a huge indoor snow-covered ski slope complete with regular snowfall amid the sultry heat of the Gulf. Accredited skiers and snowboarders can use five runs of varying height, steepness and difficulty, including the world's first indoor black run. There's also a Snow School ski academy for beginners and improvers, as well as a twin-track bobsled ride, a chairlift, the "Snow Bullet" zipline, snow cavern and adventure trail, plus toboganing and snowman-building opportunities. Ski Dubai also has a troupe of resident King and Gentoo penguins. A couple can be seen for free from the mall during the regular "March of the Penguins" (every 2hr on the hour), or at closer quarters on a full-blown "Penguin Encounter" (see page 117).

Shops

The Camel Company

MAP P.66, POCKET MAP K16
Souk Madinat Jumeirah ☏ 04 368 6048,
Ⓦ camelcompany.ae. Daily 10am–11pm.
Dubai's cutest selection of stuffed
toy camels, plus camel mugs, camel
cards, camel T-shirts and so on.
Other branches at Dubai Mall and
Ibn Battuta Mall.

Gallery One

MAP P.66, POCKET MAP K16
Souk Madinat Jumeirah Ⓦ g-1.com. Daily
10am–11pm.
Citywide chain selling a good
range of superb limited-edition
photographs of Dubai as well as
other fine-art photography and
superior postcards. Other branches
at Dubai Mall, Souk Al Bahar and
JBR Walk.

Gold and Diamond Park

MAP P.66, POCKET MAP L18
Sheikh Zayed Rd between interchanges
3 and 4. FGB metro ☏ 04 362 7777,
Ⓦ goldanddiamondpark.com. Fri 4–10pm,
Sat–Thurs 10am–10pm.
This low-key little mall is the place
to come if you want diamonds,
which retail here for up to half the
price you'd expect to pay back home.
You'll also find a few other precious
stones and platinum jewellery for
sale, plus a small amount of gold.
Some places can also knock up
custom-made designs.

Harvey Nichols

MAP P.66, POCKET MAP J18
Mall of the Emirates. Mall of the Emirates
metro ☏ 04 409 8888, Ⓦ harveynichols.
com. Daily 10am–10pm (Thurs–Sat until
midnight).
The flagship shop of one of
Dubai's flagship malls, this
suave, minimalist three-storey
department store offers a vast
array of international labels,
including British classics like
Vivienne Westwood and
Alexander McQueen.

Al Jaber Gallery

MAP P.66, POCKET MAP K18
Mall of the Emirates. Mall of the Emirates
metro ☏ 04 341 4103, Ⓦ aljabergallery.
ae. Daily 10am–10pm (Thurs–Sat until
midnight).
Dubai's leading purveyor of low-
grade Arabian "handicrafts". Look
hard enough and you might find
some half-decent stuff, including
attractive old traditional wooden
boxes and coffee pots, though the
shop is perhaps best regarded as a
source of hilarious kitsch. Kids will
love it. Other branches at Deira
City Centre, Dubai Mall, Souk al
Bahar, Souk Madinat Jumeirah,
Marina Mall and Ibn Battuta Mall.

Mall of the Emirates

MAP P.66, POCKET MAP J18–K18
Interchange 4, Sheikh Zayed Rd. Mall of
the Emirates metro Ⓦ malloftheemirates.
com. Daily 10am–10pm (Thurs–Sat until
midnight).
Among the best one-stop shopping
destinations in the city (see page
67), with around five hundred
stores to browse, good places to
eat and drink, and the surreal
snow-covered slopes of Ski Dubai
to ogle.

Pride of Kashmir

MAP P.66, POCKET MAP J18
Souk Madinat Jumeirah Ⓦ prideofkashmir.
com. Daily 10am–11pm.
One of the city's leading
handicrafts chains, more upmarket
than Al Jaber Gallery (see above)
but perfectly affordable. Stock
usually includes carpets and
kilims alongside assorted antiques,
pashminas and traditional-style
wooden furniture. There's a second
branch at Souk al Bahar.

Souk Madinat Jumeirah

MAP P.66, POCKET MAP K16
Madinat Jumeirah Ⓦ madinatjumeirah.
com. Daily 10am–11pm.
At the heart of the Madinat
Jumeirah, this superb re-creation
of a "traditional" souk serves up a
beguiling mix of shopping, eating

The Camel Company

and drinking opportunities. Like all good bazaars, the layout is mazy and disorienting, although you'll never be far from where you want to be. Shops include branches of Pride of Kashmir, The Camel Company and Gallery One (see opposite).

Restaurants

Après

MAP P.66, POCKET MAP J18
Mall of the Emirates. Mall of the Emirates metro ⓣ 04 341 2575. Daily 10am–1am .
Cool bar-restaurant with surreal views over the snowy slopes of Ski Dubai through big picture windows and a good range of international food (mains 65–195dh) – anything from boeuf bourguignon to fish and chips, plus excellent thin-crust pizzas (around 75dh). It's also a fun spot for a drink, with an extensive drinks selection and kick-ass cocktails.

La Parrilla

MAP P.66, POCKET MAP L15
25th floor, Jumeirah Beach Hotel, Jumeirah Rd ⓣ 04 432 3232, ⓦ bit.ly/ LaParrillaDubai. Daily 6–11.30pm.
Perched atop the *Jumeirah Beach Hotel*, this Argentinian-themed steakhouse boasts superb views of the Burj al Arab, excellent Argentinian, Australian and Wagyu steaks (180–310dh) and an appealing splash of Latin atmosphere, with live music and tango dancers nightly – ask nicely and the manageress might even sing you a song.

Pai Thai

MAP P.66, POCKET MAP K15
Dar al Masyaf Hotel, Madinat Jumeirah ⓣ 04 432 3232, ⓦ jumeirah.com. Lunch Fri & Sun 12.30–2.45pm, dinner Sun–Thurs 6–11.15pm, Fri & Sat 6.30–11.15pm.
This beautiful Thai restaurant is one of the city's most romantic places to eat, with stunning Burj al Arab views from the candlelit terrace and live music murmuring gently in the background. Food includes all the usual Thai classics, such as spicy salads, and meat or seafood curries – not the most original menu in town, although given the setting you probably won't care. Mains 80–200dh.

Pierchic

MAP P.66, POCKET MAP K15

Al Qasr Hotel, Madinat Jumeirah ⊕ 04 432 3232, ⓦ jumeirah.com. Daily noon–3pm & 6.30–11pm.

One of the city's most spectacularly situated restaurants, perched at the end of a breezy pier jutting out in front of the grandiose *Al Qasr* hotel, and with unbeatable views of the nearby Burj al Arab, *Jumeirah Beach Hotel* and Madinat Jumeirah (try to get a table on the terrace). The mainly seafood menu has top-dollar prices to match the location, although the quality of the food is strictly average and the menu selection (Atlantic cod, organic salmon and so on) run of the mill. Mains 195–250dh.

Segreto

MAP P.66, POCKET MAP K16

Souk Madinat Jumeirah ⊕ 04 432 3232, ⓦ jumeirah.com. Sun–Thurs 3–8pm, Fri & Sat noon–8pm.

Hidden away in the depths of the Souk Madinat Jumeirah, *Segreto* ("secret") is just what its name suggests. The romantic atmosphere and classy Italian food (mains 175–190dh) make for one of the Madinat's most seductive combinations, with superb pastas and risottos, plus top-notch meat and seafood mains. Choose between a table inside the intimate dining room or nestled between wind towers on the rooftop terrace, with the Madinat waterways illuminated below.

Tortuga

MAP P.66, POCKET MAP K15

Mina A'Salam, Jumeirah Rd ⊕ 04 432 3232, ⓦ jumeirah.com. Sun–Wed noon–3pm & 6–11.30pm, Thurs–Sat noon–11.30pm.

A vibrant restaurant shining with all the warmth and colour of Mexico. The authentic taste of the food is complemented by a real Mariachi band playing lively Latin rhythms. Music is unobtrusive enough not to hinder conversation and it might just help revive you after a tiring day under the hot Dubai sun.

Zheng He

MAP P.66, POCKET MAP K15

Mina A'Salam Hotel, Madinat Jumeirah ⊕ 04 366 6730, ⓦ jumeirah.com. Daily noon–3pm & 6.30pm–12.30am.

Classy Chinese restaurant dishing up top-notch fine dining

Pierchic

(mainly Cantonese, with a splash of Szechuan). There's nothing particularly innovative about the menu (mains 90–220dh), although quality is high and the setting memorable, with seating either inside the svelte restaurant or outside on the beautiful Burj-facing terrace.

Bars

Bahri Bar

MAP P.66, POCKET MAP K15
Mina A'Salam, Madinat Jumeirah ⓣ 04 366 8888. Daily 4pm–2am (Thurs & Fri until 3am).
Superb little Arabian-style outdoor terrace, liberally scattered with canopied sofas, Moorish artefacts and Persian carpets, and offering drop-dead gorgeous views of the Burj and Madinat Jumeirah – particularly gorgeous towards sunset.

Gold on 27

MAP P.66, POCKET MAP K15
27th floor, Burj Al Arab. Jumeirah ⓣ 04 301 7600, ⓦ goldon27.com. Daily 4pm–midnight.
As the name suggests, the elegant decor in this 27th-floor bar glitters with gold elements. Located beneath the building's helipad, there's a splendid view of the city skyline. The ambiance is luxurious, chic and upscale, so don't expect to scrimp on the drinks.

Koubba

MAP P.66, POCKET MAP K16
Lobby Floor, Jumeirah Al Qasr. Jumeirah ⓣ 04 432 3232, ⓦ goldon27.com. Sat–Thurs 5pm–3am, Fri 4pm–3am.
A beautiful rooftop terrace bar overlooking a pool and gardens. With its velvet seating and arabesque awnings, you might just feel as if you've stepped back in time. It's never hectic here, so come to relax by sinking into a comfy sofa and watching the sun go down. If you happen to like shisha, the sight of smoke trailing off into the Arabian night might be quite memorable.

Skyview Bar

MAP P.66, POCKET MAP K15
Burj al Arab ⓣ 04 301 7600, ⓔ BAArestaurants@jumeirah.com. Daily: afternoon tea seatings 1pm & 4pm; drinks 7pm–1am.
Landmark bar perched near the summit of the Burj al Arab, with psychedelic decor and vast sea and city views – coming for a drink here is currently the cheapest way to see the inside of this fabulous hotel. The huge drinks list majors in cocktails (from 100dh), but also sports a decent spread of wines, spirits, mocktails and even a few beers; alternatively, go for the lavish, seven-course afternoon teas (620dh). Minimum spend of 350dh per person; reserve in advance via email.

Uptown Bar

MAP P.66, POCKET MAP L15
Jumeirah Beach Hotel, Jumeirah Rd ⓣ 04 432 3232, ⓦ jumeirahbeachhotel.com. Sat–Wed 5pm–2am, Thurs 5pm–3am, Fri 4pm–3am.
Superb views of the Burj al Arab and southern Dubai are the main draw at this place, located on the 24th floor of the *Jumeirah Beach Hotel.* There's indoor and outdoor seating, plus a reasonable drinks list, although the decor is disappointingly humdrum for such a fine location.

Club

Silk Club

MAP 66, POCKET MAP J18
Grand Excelsior Hotel. Al Barsha. ⓣ 50 179 3179, ⓦ trilogy.ae. Daily midnight–3am.
Sleek and modern, no wonder this club is gaining such popularity in Dubai. Generally on the indie, alternative side, Thursday nights are for electronic music and there's even some vintage rock in the middle of the week.

The Palm Jumeirah and Dubai Marina

Nowhere is the scale of Dubai's explosive growth as staggeringly obvious as in the far south of the city, home to the vast Palm Jumeirah artificial island and Dubai Marina development – evidence of the emirate's magical ability to turn sand into skyscrapers and raise entire new city suburbs up out of the waves. In the early 2000s this whole area was more or less desert. Then the developers moved in. By mid-decade the district had turned into the largest construction site on the planet. Ten years on and the cranes and building crews have gone, leaving a brand-new city and the world's largest man-made island in their wake, with a forest of densely packed skyscrapers lined up around the glitzy marina itself and the fronds of the Palm spreading out into the waters beyond.

Palm Jumeirah

POCKET MAP D10–G15
Monorail trains 2–3 hourly; 20dh one way, 30dh return.

Lying off the coast around 5km south of the Burj al Arab and stretching 4km out into the waters of the Arabian Gulf, The **Palm Jumeirah** – the biggest artificial island in the world – has doubled the length of the Dubai coastline at a total cost of

Palm Jumeirah

Dubai's artificial islands

For a city with aspirations of taking over the world's tourism industry, Dubai has a serious lack of one thing: **coast**. In its natural state, the emirate boasts a mere 70km of shoreline, totally insufficient for its various needs. Dubai's solution to its pressing lack of waterfront was characteristically bold: it decided to build some more. The Palm Jumeirah was just the first (and smallest) of four proposed offshore developments. Two further palm-shaped islands – the **Palm Jebel Ali**, 20km further down the coast, and the gargantuan **Palm Deira**, right next to the old city centre – were also planned, although work on both has been on hold since late 2008. The current status of the even more fanciful **The World** development is similarly uncertain. Lying around 5km off the coast, this complex of artificial islands has been constructed in the shape of an approximate map of the world. Although physical reclamation of the islands has been complete since around 2006, most of the islands remain uninhabited dots of sand in the ocean.

over US$12 billion. As its name suggests, the Palm Jumeirah is designed in the shape of a palm tree, with a central "trunk" and a series of sixteen radiating "fronds", the whole enclosed in an 11km-long breakwater, or "crescent", lined with a string of huge, upmarket resorts.

The best way to see the Palm is from the **Palm Jumeirah Monorail**, whose driverless trains shuttle along an elevated track between the *Atlantis* resort and the mainland, offering sweeping views over the Palm. The mainland terminus of the monorail connects to Palm Jumeirah station on the Dubai Tram network.

Atlantis

POCKET MAP E10–F10

Crescent Rd, Palm Jumeirah ☏ 04 426 0000, ⓦ atlantisthepalm.com. Monorail trains 2–3 hourly; 20dh one way, 30dh return. Aquaventure 330dh, or 280dh for children under 1.2m. Dolphin Bay from 950dh; includes admission to Aquaventure. The Lost Chambers daily 10am–10pm; 135dh; children aged 3–11 70dh; under-2s free.

At the furthest end of the Palm Jumeirah, the vast **Atlantis** resort

is the island's major landmark: an outlandish pink colossus perched over the sea like some kind of weird triumphal arch. What it lacks in architectural taste, it does at least partly make up for in on-site facilities and (pricey) activities. Best is the spectacular **Aquaventure** water park, featuring an adrenaline-charged array of

The Lost Chambers aquarium

rides and slides centred on the dramatic "Ziggurat", where you'll find the park's headline Leap of Faith waterslide – 27.5m tall, it catapults you at stomach-churning speed down into a transparent tunnel amid a lagoon full of sharks. There are further watery attractions at **Dolphin Bay**, next door, where you can swim with the hotel's bottlenose dolphins. However, be aware that keeping dolphins in captivity is known to be distressing to them.

Alternatively, head to **The Lost Chambers**, a sequence of halls and tunnels through the hotel's vast underground aquarium, populated by an extraordinary array of 65,000-odd tropical fish and dotted with assorted Atlantis-style "ruins".

Dubai Marina

MAP P.74, POCKET MAP A15–D16
Dubai Marina or Jumeirah Lake Towers metros.

A vast phalanx of tightly packed high-rises signals the appearance of **Dubai Marina**, Dubai's brand-new city-within-a-city, built at lightning speed since 2005. Like much of modern Dubai, the marina is a mishmash of the good, the bad and the downright ugly. Many of the high-rises are of minimal architectural distinction, and all are packed so closely together that the overall effect is of hyperactive urban development gone completely mad. The whole area feels oddly piecemeal and under-planned, while the lack of pedestrian facilities (excepting the pleasant oceanfront The Walk at JBR and Marina Walk; see page 77) means that you're unlikely to see much more of it than can be glimpsed while speeding down Sheikh Zayed Road by car or metro.

It's weirdly impressive, even so, especially by night, when darkness

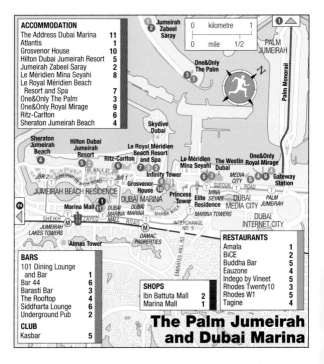

ACCOMMODATION

The Address Dubai Marina	11
Atlantis	1
Grosvenor House	10
Hilton Dubai Jumeirah Resort	5
Jumeirah Zabeel Saray	2
Le Méridien Mina Seyahi	8
Le Royal Méridien Beach Resort and Spa	7
One&Only The Palm	3
One&Only Royal Mirage	9
Ritz-Carlton	6
Sheraton Jumeirah Beach	4

BARS

101 Dining Lounge and Bar	1
Bar 44	6
Barasti Bar	3
The Rooftop	4
Siddharta Lounge	6
Underground Pub	2

CLUB

Kasbar	5

SHOPS

Ibn Battuta Mall	2
Marina Mall	1

RESTAURANTS

Amala	1
BiCE	2
Buddha Bar	5
Eauzone	4
Indego by Vineet	5
Rhodes Twenty10	3
Rhodes W1	5
Tagine	4

The Palm Jumeirah and Dubai Marina

Marina beaches

All Dubai's **beach hotels** allow non-guests to use their beaches, swimming pools and other facilities for a (usually hefty) fee, although some places close to outsiders when occupancy levels rise above a certain percentage. Rates vary from around 200dh per day midweek at the *Sheraton Jumeirah Beach* to upwards of 500dh at places like *Al Qasr* and the *Ritz-Carlton*. Given the wallet-emptying amounts of money involved, many people prefer to head to the stretch of **free beach** between the *Sheraton* and *Hilton* hotels, which has plenty of white sand to loll about on, though there are several other free or cheap beaches. A wide range of watersports are available through either Sky & Sea (Ⓦwatersportsdubai.com) or Water Adventure Dubai (Ⓦwateradventure.ae), both located on the beach behind the *Sheraton* hotel, with activities including windsurfing, sailing, kayaking, waterskiing, wake-boarding, parasailing and jet-skiing.

hides the worst examples of gimcrack design and the whole area lights up into a fabulous display of airy neon (or, if you prefer, a display of high-rise ecological catastrophe waiting to happen).

Dubai Internet and Media Cities

MAP P.74, POCKET MAP D16–E16
Nakheel metro.

Marina Beach

At the north end of Dubai Marina lie **Dubai Internet City** and **Dubai Media City** – the first and most successful in a string of dedicated business areas set up by the government to lure foreign firms to the city under preferential commercial terms. There's not really much to see here, though travelling up and down Sheikh Zayed Road or on the metro you

Dubai: the world's tallest city

Dubai is now officially the tallest city on the planet: at the time of writing it was home to 21 of the world's 100 highest buildings. By comparison, traditional high-rise hotspots Hong Kong and Chicago muster just six top-100 buildings apiece, while Shanghai manages just five – only one more than Abu Dhabi. The landmark example of Dubai's sky-high ambition is provided by the staggering Burj Khalifa (see page 51), while other high-rise icons include the Burj al Arab (see page 64) and the glittering Emirates Towers (see page 50), as well as less-well-known buildings such as the twin towers of the *JW Marriott Marquis Dubai* (see page 54), the world's tallest hotel.

can't fail to notice the soaring **Al Kazim Towers** – a pair of quirky skyscrapers styled after New York's iconic Chrysler Building.

Jumeirah Beach Residence and The Walk

MAP P.74, POCKET MAP A15–B15
Dubai Marina metro. ⓦ thewalkdubai.
com. Covent Garden Market open Oct–April
Wed & Thurs 5pm–midnight, Fri & Sat
10am–9pm.

Most of Dubai Marina's tourist development is focused on the string of luxurious **beachside hotels** which established themselves here when the coast was largely undeveloped, but now find themselves tragically hemmed in by densely packed high-rises on all sides. Notable among these is the unlovely **Jumeirah Beach Residence (JBR)**: a 1.7km-long sprawl of forty high-rises with living space for ten thousand people. The JBR's one redeeming feature is **The Walk at JBR**, an attractive promenade lined with boutiques,

Marina Walk

Starbucks, Ibn Battuta Mall

pizzerias, coffee shops, burger joints and fast-food outlets – one of the very few places in the new city which positively encourages people to get out of their cars.

Marina Walk

MAP P.74, POCKET MAP B16–C16
Marina or Jumeirah Lake Towers metros.
Dubai's **marina** is actually a man-made sea inlet, lined with luxury yachts and fancy speedboats, which snakes inland behind the JBR, running parallel with the coast for around 1.5km. Encircling the water is the attractive pedestrianized promenade known as **Marina Walk**, its long straggle of waterfront cafés and restaurants enjoyably lively after dark. Presiding over the northern sea inlet into the marina is the quirky **Infinity Tower** (330m), the latest in Dubai's increasingly long list of iconic skyscrapers and instantly recognizable thanks to its distinctively twisted outline, which rotates through 90 degrees from base to summit – a bit like the famous Turning Tower in Malmö, Sweden.

Various kiosks around Marina Walk offer a mix of expensive **boat** charters alongside much cheaper dhow cruises for those who want to take to the water.

Ibn Battuta Mall

POCKET MAP A16
Between interchanges 5 and 6 (exits 25 and 27), Sheikh Zayed Rd. Ibn Battuta metro ⓦ ibnbattutamall.com. Daily 10am–1am (dining until 2am).
The outlandish, mile-long **Ibn Battuta Mall** is undoubtedly Dubai's wackiest shopping experience. The mall is themed in six different sections after some of the places – Morocco, Andalucia, Tunisia, Persia, India and China – visited by the famous Arab traveller Ibn Battuta. Highlights include a life-sized elephant complete with mechanical mahout (rider), a twilit Tunisian village and a full-sized Chinese junk, while the lavishness of some of the decoration would seem more appropriate on a Rajput palace or a Persian grand mosque than a motorway mall.

Shops

Ibn Battuta Mall

POCKET MAP A16
Between interchanges 5 and 6,
Sheikh Zayed Rd. Ibn Battuta metro
Ⓦ ibnbattutamall.com. Daily 10am–1am
(dining until 2am).

This Ibn Battuta-inspired mall is
worth a visit for its stunning decor
alone – although as a shopping
experience it's a bit underpowered.
Shops include a handy Borders
bookstore, a well-stocked branch
of the local Toy Store chain and
the chic Ginger & Lace ladieswear
boutique – and it's worth a look
at the entertaining Daiso in the
Andalucia court, a kind of Japanese
pound shop with everything for
under 10dh.

Marina Mall

MAP P.74, POCKET MAP B16
Sheikh Zayed Rd. Jumeirah Lakes Towers
metro Ⓦ marinamall.ae. Daily 10am–10pm
(Thurs & Fri until midnight).

Dubai's newest and swankiest
mall, with a big selection of
mainly upmarket outlets – the big
central atrium looks like a kind

Eauzone

of postmodern temple of designer
brands. There's also a good selection
of cafés in the water-facing side and
in the attached Pier 7 tower.

Restaurants

Amala

MAP P.74, POCKET MAP C13
Jumeirah Zabeel Saray hotel, Palm
Jumeirah Ⓣ 04 453 0444, Ⓦ jumeirah.com.
Fri & Sat 1–4pm & 6pm–1am, Sun–Thurs
6pm–1am.

The most popular of the *Zabeel
Saray's* stunning collection of
restaurants, as opulently decorated
as a Bollywood film set and with
good, quite reasonably priced food
(mains 75–175dh), and a mainly
North Indian menu featuring
classics like butter chicken and
rogan josh alongside a good
vegetarian selection.

Bice

MAP P.74, POCKET MAP B15
Hilton Jumeirah Beach Resort, Dubai
Marina. Jumeirah Beach Residence 1 tram
station Ⓣ 04 318 2520, Ⓦ facebook.com/
bicedubai. Daily 12.30–3pm & 7–11.30pm.

Polished modern Italian –reckoned
by some to be the best in the
southern city – serving up tasty pizzas
and pastas (75–125dh) bursting with
fresh ingredients and flavours, plus
a mix of more elaborate meat and
seafood mains (105–215dh).

Buddha Bar

MAP P.74, POCKET MAP C16
Grosvenor House Hotel, Dubai Marina.
DAMAC Properties metro Ⓣ 04 317 6000,
Ⓦ buddhabar.com. Daily 7pm–midnight
(bar until 1/2am).

Modelled after the famous Parisian
joint, this superb bar-restaurant
is a sight in its own right: a huge,
sepulchral space hung with dozens
of red-lantern chandeliers. The
menu features a fine array of
Japanese and pan-Asian cooking
– pricey (mains 180–295dh), but
worth it for the ambience. Advance
reservations recommended.

Indego by Vineet

Eauzone

MAP P.74, POCKET MAP E15
Arabian Courtyard, One&Only Royal Mirage, Dubai Marina. Palm Jumeirah tram station ☎ 04 399 9999, ⓦ royalmirage. oneandonlyresorts.com. Daily noon–3.30pm & 7–11.30pm.
Regularly voted Dubai's most romantic restaurant, with seating amid the beautifully floodlit waters of one of the hotel's swimming pools and a short but sweet menu (mains 135–200dh) of pan-Asian classics alongside more contemporary creations – anything from miso-glazed black cod to Earl Grey tea mousse. Reserve ahead.

Indego by Vineet

MAP P.74, POCKET MAP C15
Grosvenor House Hotel, Dubai Marina. DAMAC Properties metro ☎ 04 317 6000, ⓦ indegobyvineet.com. Daily 7pm–midnight.
Overseen by Vineet Bhatia, India's first Michelin-starred chef, this stylish restaurant showcases his contemporary Indian cooking, blending subcontinental and international ingredients and techniques to unusual effect. Mains 125–320dh.

Rhodes Twenty10

MAP P.74, POCKET MAP C15
Le Royal Méridien, Dubai Marina. DAMAC Properties metro ☎ 04 316 5505, ⓦ leroyalmeridien-dubai.com. Daily except Mon 7pm–midnight. Fri & Sat 2.30–5pm afternoon tea.
Casual and affordable, Gary Rhodes' second Dubai restaurant features an excellent range of "European-inspired cuisine infused with a touch of the Middle East" alongside British classics like grilled kidneys and fish 'n' chips with mushy peas. Mains 95–190dh.

Rhodes W1

MAP P.74, POCKET MAP C15
Grosvenor House Hotel, Dubai Marina. DAMAC Properties metro ☎ 04 317 6000, ⓦ rw1-dubai.com. Daily 7pm–midnight.
Gary Rhodes' original Dubai restaurant has recently relaunched with a slightly more laidback atmosphere and crisp white decor. The seasonally changing menu (mains 130–210dh) features contemporary remakes of old-school favourites like chicken Kiev, shepherds' pie and braised oxtail, and they also do a fine afternoon tea (2.30–5pm; 195dh).

Rhodes W1

Tagine

MAP P.74, POCKET MAP E15
The Palace, One&Only Royal Mirage, Dubai Marina. Media City tram station ☎ 04 399 9999, Ⓦ royalmirage.oneandonlyresorts. com. Daily except Mon 7–10pm.
Sumptuous little Moroccan restaurant, the beautiful Moorish decor complemented by authentic North African cooking including classics like *pastilla* (pigeon pie), *tangia* and a selection of delicious tagines. Mains around 105–150dh.

Bars

101 Dining Lounge and Bar

MAP P.74, POCKET MAP C14
One&Only The Palm, Palm Jumeirah ☎ 04 440 1030, Ⓦ thepalm.oneandonlyresorts. com. Daily 11.30am–2am.
Overlooking the swish new *One&Only The Palm*'s private marina, *101*'s big draws are its gorgeous terrace over the water outside (live DJ most evenings) and stunning views across to the marina's skyscrapers opposite.

Bar 44

MAP P.74, POCKET MAP C15
44th floor, Grosvenor House Hotel, Dubai Marina. DAMAC Properties metro ☎ 04 317 6000, Ⓦ grosvenorhousedubai.com. Daily 5.30pm–2.30am (Thurs until 3am).
This svelte contemporary bar offers peerless 360-degree views of the entire marina development, with twinkling high-rises stretching away in every direction and a big selection of wallet-emptying champagnes and cool cocktails.

Barasti Bar

MAP P.74, POCKET MAP D15
Le Méridien Mina Sehayi, Dubai Marina. Mina Seyahi tram station ☎ 04 318 1313 Ⓦ barastibeach.com. Sun–Wed 10am–1.30am, Thurs & Fri 10am–3am, Sat 9am–1.30am.
Fun, two-level beachside bar popular with an eclectic crowd. Downstairs is usually more Ibiza chill-out, with ambient music, shisha and loungers on the sand; the pubbier upstairs is generally noisier, with live DJs and a party atmosphere.

The Rooftop

MAP P.74, POCKET MAP E15
Arabian Court, One&Only Royal Mirage, Dubai Marina. Media City tram station ☎ 04 399 9999, ⓦ royalmirage. oneandonlyresorts.com. Daily 5pm–2am.
One of Dubai's ultimate Orientalist fantasies, with seductive Moorish decor, cushion-strewn pavilions, silver-tray tables and other assorted Arabian artefacts. A smooth live DJ adds to the *One Thousand and One Nights* ambience.

Siddharta Lounge

MAP P.74, POCKET MAP C16
Tower Two, Grosvenor House Hotel. Dubai Marina metro ☎ 04 317 6000, ⓦ siddhartalounge.com. Dinner Sat–Wed 5pm–midnight, Thurs & Fri 5pm–12.30am; Shisha 5–11.15pm.
Swanky new venue with a cool poolside terrace and bar outside, as well as a "palm area" with shisha lounge within – all snowy-white decor with the occasional gold armchair. There's also a good selection of Asian and Mediterranean-style light meals and snacks.

The Rooftop

Underground Pub

MAP P.74, POCKET MAP C15
Habtoor Grand Resort, ground level. Royal Meridian 1 metro ☎ 04 408 4257, ⓦ tinyurl.com/UndergroundPub. Daily noon–3am.
An underground-themed classic British pub, fisn 'n' chips, quiz night and all. The bar itself is within a structure resembling an underground rail car – a cosy portal to London from the streets of Dubai. Packed during sporting seasons.

Club

Kasbar

MAP P.74, POCKET MAP D15
One & Only Royal Mirage, Al Sufouh 2.Royal Meridian 1 metro ☎ 04 399 9999, ⓦ tinyurl.com/KasbarClub. Daily noon–3am.
A multi-level venue situated in the One & Only Royal Mirage Palace, on the top two levels you can enjoy come cool night-time air on the terraces. DJs play an eclectic mix of old and new arabic hits from around the Gulf.

THE PALM JUMEIRAH AND DUBAI MARINA

Sharjah

Just 10km north up the coast, the city of Sharjah seems at first sight like simply an extension of Dubai, with whose northern suburbs it now merges seamlessly in an ugly concrete sprawl. Physically, the two cities may have virtually fused into one, but culturally they remain light years apart. Sharjah has a distinctively different flavour, having clung much more firmly to its traditional Islamic roots, exemplified by a fine array of museums devoted to various aspects of Islamic culture and local Emirati life. These include the world-class Museum of Islamic Civilization, the excellent Sharjah Art Gallery, the impressive Sharjah Heritage Museum, and the engaging Al Mahatta aviation museum. Other attractions include the massive Blue Souk, one of the largest in the UAE, and Souq al Arsa, one of the prettiest.

Sharjah Museum of Islamic Civilization

MAP P.84
Corniche St ☎ 06 565 5455, Ⓦ sharjahmuseums.ae. Sat–Thurs 8am–8pm, Fri 4–8pm. 10dh.

The main reason for trekking out to Sharjah is to visit the superb **Sharjah Museum of Islamic Civilization**, which occupies the beautifully restored waterfront Souk al Majara building, topped with a distinctive golden dome. The museum is spread over two levels. Downstairs, the **Abu Bakr Gallery of Islamic Faith** has extensive displays on the elaborate rituals associated with the traditional Haj pilgrimage to Mecca, while the **Ibn al Haitham Gallery of Science and Technology** showcases the extensive contributions made by Arab scholars to scientific innovation over the centuries. The first floor of the museum is devoted to four galleries offering a chronological overview of **Islamic arts and crafts**, with superb displays of historic manuscripts, ceramics, glass, armour, woodwork, textiles and jewellery. Exhibits

include the first-ever map of the then known world (ie Eurasia), created by Moroccan cartographer Al Shereef al Idrisi in 1099 – a surprisingly accurate document, although slightly baffling at first sight since it's oriented upside down, with south at the top.

Sharjah Creek

MAP P.84
Sharjah's broad **Creek** describes a leisurely parabola around the northern edge of the city centre before terminating in the expansive Khaled Lagoon. Despite being long since eclipsed by Dubai's various ports, Sharjah's Creek still sees a considerable amount of commercial shipping both modern and traditional, usually with a few old-fashioned wooden dhows moored up on the far side of the water beneath a long line of spiky gantries.

Sharjah Art Museum

MAP P.84
Clearly signed off Corniche St, or access from Al Burj Ave, behind Al Hisn fort ☎ 06 568 8222, Ⓦ sharjahmuseums.ae. Sat–

Thurs 8am–8pm, Fri 4–8pm. Free.
Occupying a large modern wind-towered building, the **Sharjah Art Museum** is the major showpiece in Sharjah's attempts to position itself as a serious player in the international art scene. Temporary exhibitions of varying quality feature on the ground floor.

Upstairs, the museum's new permanent gallery of modern Arabian art holds a wide range of works created in the past four decades from countries across the region in an eclectic range of styles and media – all technically proficient, although none lingers long in the memory.

Al Hisn Fort

MAP P.84
Al Burj Ave ☏ 06 568 5500,
🌐 sharjahmuseums.ae. 10dh. Fri 4pm–8pm, Sat–Thurs 8am–8pm.
At the heart of the city is the modest **Al Hisn Fort** of 1820, the most enduring symbol of old Sharjah, formerly home to the ruling Al Qassimi family, although it's now ignominiously hemmed in by ugly apartment blocks. The fort reopened in 2014 after

prolonged renovations and now looks neater, shinier and an awful lot cleaner than it ever did in the past, with a series of displays dotted around various rooms and a few atmospheric photographs of the fort in former years.

Heritage Area

MAP P.84
The area west of Al Hisn Fort was formerly the heart of old Sharjah, an old-fashioned quarter of traditional Emirati houses arranged around a sequence of spacious, lopsided squares and labyrinthine alleyways, and enclosed in a long section of reconstructed city wall. The entire area has now been meticulously renovated and relaunched as the city's so-called **Heritage Area**, home to several interesting museums and the Souq al Arsa.

Souq al Arsa and around

MAP P.84
Heritage Area. Most shops open 9/10am–1/2pm & 4/5–8pm (closed Fri morning).
The **Souq al Arsa**, which bounds the northern side of the Heritage Area, is far and away the prettiest

Al Hisn Fort

in Sharjah. The souk is centred around an atmospheric central pillared courtyard, flanked by the personable little *Al Arsaha Public Coffee House* (see opposite), beyond which radiates an intriguing tangle of alleyways. The coral-stone shops are stuffed full of all sorts of colourful local handicrafts as well as an eclectic selection of curios and collectibles.

Tucked away around the back (north) side of the Souq al Arsa is the attractive **Majlis Ibrahim Mohammed al Madfa**, topped by a diminutive round wind tower, said to be the only one in the UAE.

Bait al Naboodah

MAP P.84

Opposite the Souq al Arsa, Heritage Area ☎ 06 568 1738, ⓦ sharjahmuseums.ae. Sat–Thurs 8am–8pm, Fri 4–8pm. 10dh.

Situated in an atmospheric old house, the **Bait al Naboodah** offers an interesting re-creation of traditional family life in Sharjah. The main draw is the rambling two-storey building itself, one of the most attractive in the UAE, arranged around a spacious central courtyard. Only the rooms on the ground floor are open, including a string of bedrooms furnished in traditional Gulf style.

Sharjah Heritage Museum

MAP P.84

Heritage Area ☎ 06 568 0006, ⓦ sharjahmuseums.ae. Sat–Thurs 8am–8pm, Fri 4–8pm. 10dh.

The excellent **Sharjah Heritage Museum** is one of the best collections of its kind anywhere in the UAE. Wide-ranging and well-explained exhibits cover all the usual bases – traditional dress, architecture, social customs, the pearling trade and so on – with many insights into lesser-known local customs en route.

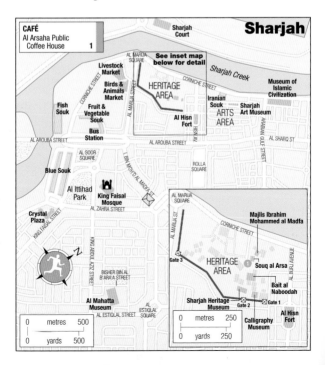

Blue Souk

Blue Souk

MAP P.84
King Faisal St, 1km west of the city centre (about 10dh by taxi). Most shops open roughly 10am–10pm, although many close around 1–4pm.

The huge **Blue Souk** (officially known as the Central Souk) occupies an enormous, eye-catching and ungainly pair of buildings topped by myriad wind towers and clad in brilliant blue tiling. The souk is best known for its numerous carpet shops, which stock a vast range of Persian and other rugs (usually) at significantly lower prices than in Dubai.

Al Mahatta Museum

MAP P.84
Bisher bin al Bara'a St (Street 23), off King Abdul Aziz St (around 15dh by taxi from the centre) ☎ 06 573 3079, ⓦ sharjahmuseums.ae. Sat–Thurs 8am–8pm, Fri 4–8pm. 10dh.

Devoted to the history of aviation in Sharjah, the **Al Mahatta Museum** is unexpectedly absorbing. It occupies the buildings of what was until 1977 the city's airport, complete with aircraft hangar and air traffic control tower (the runway was incorporated into what is now King Abdul Aziz Street). The cavernous **hangar** contains five antique planes dating from the 1930s to the 1950s, while the remainder of the museum occupies the old airport **rest house**, with fascinating displays about the first commercial flights to Sharjah (launched in 1932 by Imperial Airways) and other exhibits.

Café

Al Arsaha Public Coffee House

MAP P.84
Souq al Arsa. Daily 8am–9pm.

This quaint little café offers a beguiling window on local life, with attractive decor in traditional Arabian style and an entertaining local clientele. It's a good place for a glass of mint tea or a cup of coffee, and they also serve up mountainous, spicy biriyanis (chicken, mutton or fish; 15dh).

Al Ain

For a complete change of pace and scenery, a day-trip out to the sedate desert city of Al Ain, some 130km inland (a two-hour minibus ride) from Dubai on the border with Oman, offers the perfect antidote to the rip-roaring pace of life on the coast. The UAE's fourth-largest city and only major inland settlement, Al Ain – and the twin city of Buraimi, on the Omani side of the border – grew up around the string of six oases whose densely packed swathes of palms still dot the modern city. The city served as an important staging post on trading routes between Oman and the Gulf, a fact attested to by the numerous forts that dot the area and by the rich archeological remains found in the vicinity, evidence of continuous settlement dating back to Neolithic times.

Al Ain National Museum and around

MAP P.88
Off Zayed bin Sultan St. Closed for renovation at the time of writing.

The old-fashioned **Al Ain National Museum** is well worth a look before diving into the rest of the city. The first section sports the usual dusty displays on local life and culture, while the second offers a comprehensive overview of the archeology of the UAE.

Right next to the museum, the **Sultan bin Zayed Fort** (or Eastern Fort) is one of the eighteen or so scattered around Al Ain. The picturesque three-towered structure is best known as the childhood home of Sheikh Zayed bin Sultan al Nahyan (ruled 1966–2004), who oversaw the transformation of the emirate from impoverished Arabian backwater into today's oil-rich contemporary city-state.

Al Ain Oasis

MAP P.88
Between Al Ain St and Zayed bin Sultan St, south of the centre. Daily sunrise–sunset. Free.

A dusty green wall of palms announces the beautiful **Al Ain Oasis**, with a mazy network of little walled lanes running between the densely planted thickets of trees including an estimated 150,000-odd date palms. There are eight entrances dotted around the perimeter of the oasis, although given the disorienting tangle of roads within, you're unlikely to end up coming out where you entered.

Al Ain Souk

MAP P.88
Immediately in front of the bus station. Most stalls/shops open daily approx 8am–noon/1pm & 4/5–8pm (Fri 4/5–8pm only).

Al Ain Souk is home to the city's main meat, fruit and vegetable market. Housed in a long, functional warehouse-style building, the souk is stocked with the usual picturesque piles of produce, prettiest at the structure's west end, where Indian traders sit enthroned amid huge mounds of fruit and vegetables.

Al Ain Palace Museum

MAP P.88
Al Ain St, on the western side of Al Ain Oasis ☎ 03 751 7755, ⓦ bit.ly/AlAinPalace. Sat, Sun & Tues–Thurs 8.30am–7.30pm, Fri 3.30–7.30pm, closed Mon. Free.

A khanjar (dagger), Al Ain National Museum

The **Al Ain Palace Museum** occupies one of the various forts around Al Ain owned by the ruling Nahyan family of Abu Dhabi. The sprawling complex is pleasant enough, with rambling, orangey-pink buildings arranged around a sequence of five courtyards and small gardens, although the palace's thirty-odd rooms, including assorted bedrooms, *majlis* and a small school, aren't particularly interesting.

Jahili Fort

MAP P.88.
120th St, off Sultan bin Zayed al Awwal St. Sat, Sun & Tues–Thurs 9am–5pm, Fri 3–5pm, closed Mon. Free.
Of Al Ain's various mud-brick forts, **Jahili Fort**, built in 1898, is easily the most impressive, with a fine battlemented main tower and a spacious central courtyard. The much-photographed circular tower on the northern side – with four levels of diminishing size, each topped with a line of triangular battlements – probably predates the rest of the fort. Jahili Fort is also home to the excellent little **Mubarak bin London** exhibition, devoted to the life of legendary explorer

Wilfred Thesiger (1910–2003). Thesiger – or Mubarak bin London (the "Blessed Son of London") as he was known to his Arab friends – stayed at the fort in the late 1940s at the end of one of the two pioneering journeys across the deserts of the Empty Quarter which later formed the centrepiece of *Arabian Sands*, his classic narrative of Middle Eastern exploration.

Hili Gardens and Archeological Park

About 8km north of the city. Daily 9.30am–6.30pm. Free.
The **Hili Gardens and Archeological Park** is the site of one of the most important archeological sites in the UAE – many finds from here are displayed in the Al Ain Museum, which also provides a good explanation of their significance. The main surviving structure is the so-called "**Hili Grand Tomb**", a circular mausoleum dating from the third century BC, made from large, finely cut and fitted slabs of stones. A quaint carving of two people framed by a pair of long-horned oryx decorates the rear entrance.

Al Ain Zoo

Off Nahyan al Awwal St, around 7km southwest of the centre ☎ 800 966, ⓦ alainzoo.ae. Daily: Oct–April 9am–8pm; May–Sept 4–10pm. 30dh; children aged 3–12 10dh; under-3s free.

The excellent **Al Ain Zoo** is a guaranteed crowd-pleaser for both kids and adults. There are over four thousand animals here, humanely housed in large open pens spread around the very spacious grounds. Inmates include plenty of African fauna – big cats, giraffes, zebras and rhinos (including rare South African white lions and Nubian giraffes) – along with numerous Arabian animals and birds.

Camel Souk

Off the Oman road, near the Bawadi mall, about 9km from the city centre.

Al Ain's old-fashioned **Camel Souk** (actually just a series of pens in the open desert) is worth a visit, despite being a bit tricky to find, attracting a lively crowd of local camel-fanciers haggling over dozens of dromedaries lined up for sale. The souk is busiest in the mornings before around 10am, although low-key trading may continue throughout the day. Be aware that there are some very pushy traders here who may demand massively inflated tips for showing you around or allowing you to take photographs of their animals. Always agree a sum in advance.

Jebel Hafeet

30km south of Al Ain on the Omani border. Taxis cost around 100dh.

The soaring 1180m **Jebel Hafeet** (or Hafit), the second-highest mountain in the UAE, is a popular retreat for locals wanting to escape the heat of the desert plains. You can drive to the top in half an hour or less along an excellent road, from

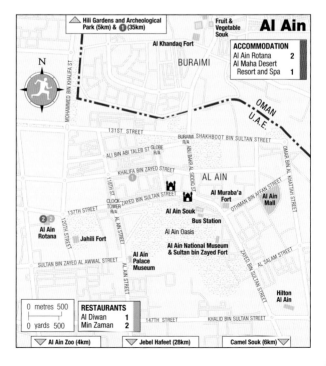

Dubai Desert Conservation Reserve

where there are peerless views over the surrounding Hajar mountains. The outdoor terrace at the *Mercure Grand* hotel, perched just below the summit, makes a memorable – if often surprisingly chilly – spot for a drink.

Dubai Desert Conservation Reserve

E66 highway, around 50km from Dubai and 75km from Al Ain Ⓦ ddcr.org.

For a taste of real, unadulterated UAE desert, it's well worth a visit to the superb **Dubai Desert Conservation Reserve**. The reserve encloses 250 square kilometres of shifting dunes which serve as a refuge for over thirty local mammal and reptile species, including rare and endangered oryx and Arabian mountain gazelle. Tours can be arranged through Arabian Adventures, Lama, Travco and Alpha (see page 111). Alternatively, you can stay in the reserve at the idyllic but wickedly expensive *Al Maha* resort (see page 104).

Restaurants

Al Diwan

MAP P.88
Khalifa bin Zayed St Ⓣ 03 764 4445.
Daily 10am–12.30am.

Rustic-looking restaurant with very cheery staff and a menu of Lebanese, Iranian and European classics – grilled pigeon, kebabs, assorted mezze and a wide selection of (pricier) seafood. Most mains 35–70dh.

Min Zaman

MAP P.88
Al Ain Rotana hotel Ⓣ 03 754 5111,
Ⓦ rotana.com/alainrotana. Mon–Fri 6pm–3am.

The swankiest Lebanese restaurant in town, with a classy range of authentic dishes (mains 60–80dh). Sit either in the attractive dining room or on the terrace, listening to the resident oud player.

Abu Dhabi

The capital of the UAE, Abu Dhabi is the very model of a modern Gulf petro-city: thoroughly contemporary, shamelessly wealthy and decidedly staid. Abu Dhabi's lightning change from obscure fishing village into modern city-state within the past thirty years is perhaps the most dramatic of the region's stories of oil-driven transformation, although for the casual visitor the city is mainly interesting for how it contrasts with its more famous neighbour – an Arabian Washington to Dubai's Las Vegas. Abu Dhabi's two stand out attractions are the stunning Sheikh Zayed Mosque, one of the world's largest and most extravagant places of Islamic worship, and the ultra-opulent *Emirates Palace Hotel*. Other draws include the memorable new souk at the World Trade Center, and the contrastingly traditional Heritage Village, offering superb views of Abu Dhabi's long waterfront Corniche.

Emirates Palace Hotel

MAP P.92
Corniche Rd West ☎ 02 690 9000,
ⓦ emiratespalace.com.

Emirates Palace Hotel

Standing in splendour at the western end of the city is the vast **Emirates Palace Hotel**. Opened in 2005, it was intended to rival Dubai's *Burj al Arab* – although in fact the two buildings could hardly be more different. Driveways climb up through the grounds to the main entrance, which sits in an elevated position above the sea and surrounding gardens. It's impressively stage-managed, although the quasi-Arabian design seems pedestrian and the only really unusual thing about the building is its sheer size: 1km in length, 114 domes, 140 elevators, 2000 staff and so on. The **interior** is a lot more memorable, centred on a dazzling central atrium, with vast quantities of marble and huge chandeliers. Direcly behind is the **Presidential Palace**. Completed in 2015, it cost almost half a billion US dollars to build. Within the compound, the **Palace of the Nation** recently opened to the public. It includes a room filled with items gifted to the

UAE president as well as 50,000 books and manuscripts.

The Corniche

MAP P.92

Driving through Abu Dhabi's suburban sprawl, it's easy not to notice that the city is built on an island – at least until you emerge on the expansive **Corniche**, the sweeping waterfront road that runs for the best part of 5km along Abu Dhabi's western edge. The road is lined by spacious gardens on either side and flanked by a long line of glass-clad high-rises which both encapsulate the city's internationalist credentials and provide Abu Dhabi with its most memorable views.

Heritage Village

MAP P.92
Breakwater ☏ 02 681 4455, ⓦ torath.ae. Sat–Thurs 9am–4pm, Fri 3.30–9pm. Free.
Dramatically situated on the Breakwater – a small protuberance of reclaimed land jutting out from the southern end of the Corniche – the **Heritage Village** offers a slice of traditional Abu Dhabi done up for visiting coach parties. The "village" consists of a line of picturesque *barasti* huts, including several **workshops** where local artisans – carpenters, potters, brass-makers and so on – can sometimes be seen at work, although the main attraction is the spectacular view over the water to the skyscrapers lining the Corniche.

Marina Mall

MAP P.92

The Corniche

Marina Village, Breakwater ⓦ marinamall.ae. Daily 10am–10pm, Thurs & Fri until midnight.
Dominating the centre of the Breakwater, the large **Marina Mall** is a top shopping destination, and also offers fine views of the Corniche. These are best appreciated from the soaring **Burj al Marina** tower at the back of the mall, which you can visit for the price of an expensive drink at the 41st-floor *Colombiano* coffee shop.

Qasr al Hosn and around

MAP P.92
Al Nasr St (5th St) ⓦ quasaralhosn.ae. Sat–Thurs 9am–7pm, Fri noon–10pm. 30dh adult, 15dh child.
More or less at the very centre of Abu Dhabi sits **Qasr Al Hosn** ("The

Abu Dhabi transport

Regular express **buses** (5.30am–11.30pm; every 30min; 2hr–2hr 30min; 30dh) run from Al Ghubaiba bus station in Bur Dubai and Ibn Battuta metro station to Abu Dhabi's main bus station, about 3km inland from the city centre. A convenient alternative is to take a **tour** from Dubai. Numerous companies offer Abu Dhabi day-trips (see page 111), generally costing around 250dh. Abu Dhabi's various attractions are very spread out, but there are plenty of metered **taxis** around town (flag fare 3.50dh).

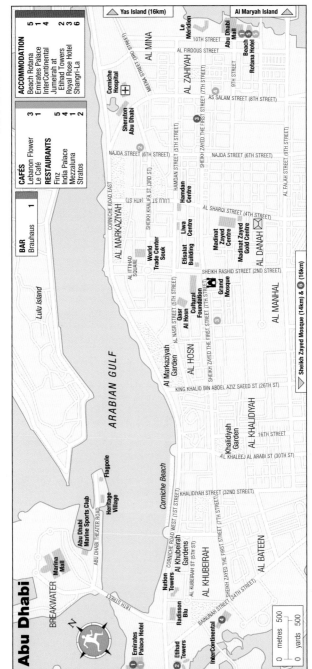

Abu Dhabi

ACCOMMODATION	
Beach Rotana	5
Emirates Palace	1
InterContinental	4
Jumeirah at Etihad Towers	2
Royal Rose Hotel	3
Shangri-La	6

CAFÉS	
Lebanon Flower	3
Le Café	1

RESTAURANTS	
Finz	5
India Palace	4
Mezzaluna	1
Stratos	2

BAR	
Brauhaus	1

Yas Island (16km)

Al Maryah Island

Le Meridien

Abu Dhabi Mall

Beach Rotana Hotel

10TH STREET

9TH STREET

MEENA STREET (3RD STREET)

AL MINA

AL FIRDOUS STREET

AL ZAHIYAH

AS SALAM STREET (8TH STREET)

Corniche Hospital

Sheraton Abu Dhabi

SHEIKH KHALIFA ST (7TH STREET)

SHEIKH ZAYED THE FIRST STREET (7TH STREET)

NAJDA STREET (6TH STREET)

HAMDAN STREET (5TH STREET)

NAJDA STREET (6TH STREET)

AL FALAH STREET (9TH STREET)

CORNICHE ROAD EAST

LULU ST (4TH ST)

SHEIKH KHALIFA ST (3RD ST)

Hamdan Centre

AL SHARQI STREET (4TH STREET)

AL MARKAZIYAH

World Trade Center Souk

AL ITTIHAD SQUARE

Etisalat Building

Liwa Centre

Madinat Zayed Centre

Madinat Zayed Gold Centre

AL DANAH

SHEIKH RASHID STREET (2ND STREET)

AL NASR STREET (5TH STREET)

Qasr Al Hosn

Cultural Foundation

Grand Mosque

AL HOSN

AL MANHAL

Lulu Island

ARABIAN GULF

Al Markaziyah Garden

SHEIKH ZAYED THE FIRST STREET (7TH STREET)

KING KHALID BIN ABDEL AZIZ SAEED ST (26TH ST)

Sheikh Zayed Mosque (14km) & (16km)

Khalidiyah Garden

AL KHALIDIYAH

16TH STREET

AL KHALEEJ AL ARABI ST (30TH ST)

Corniche Beach

KHALIDIYAH STREET (32ND STREET)

CORNICHE ROAD WEST (1ST STREET)

Abu Dhabi Marine Sports Club

Heritage Village

Flagpole

ABU DHABI THEATER ROAD

Nation Towers

Al Khubeirah Gardens

AL KUBEIRAH ST (5TH ST)

AL KHUBEIRAH

BAINUNAH STREET (34TH STREET)

SHEIKH ZAYED THE FIRST STREET (7TH STREET)

AL BATEEN

BREAKWATER

Marina Mall

Radisson Blu

Emirates Palace Hotel

Etihad Towers

InterContinental

18TH STREET

N

0   metres   500

0   yards   500

Louvre Abu Dhabi

Midway between Al Maryah and Yas islands, dusty Saadiyat Island is undergoing a shape-shifting transformation into one of the city's key tourist destinations. Centrepiece of the project is the vast new Louvre Abu Dhabi, opened in late 2017. Housed in a spectacular, flying saucer-shaped building designed by Jean Nouvel, it showcases a wide range of European and Middle Eastern artefacts from the collection of the famous Parisian museum. Over the next few years the Louvre is set to be joined by the Zayed National Museum and the Guggenheim Abu Dhabi.

Palace Fort"), the oldest building in Abu Dhabi. The fort started life around 1761 as a single round watchtower built to defend the only freshwater well in Abu Dhabi, and was subsequently expanded, serving as the residence of Abu Dhabi's ruling Al Nahyan family right up until 1966. After 11 years of renovation work it finally reopened in 2018.

World Trade Center and around

MAP P.92
Between Al Ittihad Square and Sheikh Khalifa St (3rd St) Ⓦ wtcad.ae. Souk daily 10am–10pm, Thurs & Fri until 11pm.
The huge **World Trade Center**, topped by a pair of shiny cylindrical skyscrapers, is one of the city's most interesting recent developments. The Center's main attraction is its marvellous **souk**, designed by Foster & Partners and offering a memorable postmodern take on the traditional Arabian bazaar.

On the southwestern side of the World Trade Center, **Al Ittihad Square** is home to an arresting sequence of oversized sculptures, including a vast cannon, enormous perfume bottle and gargantuan coffeepot – an endearingly quirky contrast to the drab surrounding architecture.

Downtown Abu Dhabi

MAP P.92

World Trade Center Souk

The area immediately east of Sheikh Rashid Street (2nd St) is the heart of downtown Abu Dhabi, and where you'll find the city's liveliest street life. The parallel **Hamdan Street** and **Sheikh Zayed the First Street** are the two major thoroughfares, each lined with identikit office blocks stacked tightly together like Lego bricks. Just south of the latter, the **Madinat Zayed Gold Centre** is Abu Dhabi's low-key equivalent to Dubai's Gold Souk, with two floors of jewellery shops selling traditional and modern designs.

Al Maryah Island

MAP P.92

Immediately beyond downtown, on the far side of a narrow sea inlet, a cluster of dramatic skyscrapers announce the city's new financial district, Al Maryah Island. Abu Dhabi's biggest and most futuristic urban development, the island is still very much a work in progress but is well worth a visit for a look at the dramatic central Abu Dhabi Global Market Square, with four massive skyscrapers surrounding

Sheikh Zayed Mosque

the distinctively anvil-shaped Abu Dhabi Global Market building, with the very chic waterside Galleria mall below.

Sheikh Zayed Mosque

15km from central Abu Dhabi, between Al Ain and Al Khaleej al Arabi roads (around 40dh by taxi) ☏ 02 419 1919, ⓦ szgmc.gov. ae. Sat–Thurs 9am–10pm, Fri 4.30–10pm (interior closed for about 30min during prayers; check ⓦ szgmc.gov.ae/en/mosque-opening-hours for times). Free guided tours: Sun–Thurs 10am, 11am & 5pm, Fri 5pm & 7pm, Sat 10am, 11am, 2pm, 5pm & 7pm.

The mighty **Sheikh Zayed Mosque** dominates all landward approaches to the city. Completed in 2007, it's one of the world's biggest – and certainly the most expensive, having taken twelve years to build at a cost of around US$500 million. It's also unusual in being one of the few mosques in the UAE **open to non-Muslims**.

The huge **exterior** is framed by four 107m-high minarets and topped with some eighty domes. Entrance to the mosque is through a vast **courtyard** – capable of accommodating some 40,000 worshippers. Flanking one side is the vast **prayer hall**, home to the world's largest carpet and biggest chandelier, although it's the extraordinary muted opulence of the design that impresses, with every surface richly carved and decorated.

Yas Island

About 30–35km from central Abu Dhabi; access either from the Dubai highway or along the road via Saadiyat Island.

On the outermost edges of the city, **Yas Island** is home to the **Yas Marina Circuit** (ⓦ yasmarinacircuit.com), which hosts the annual Abu Dhabi F1 Grand Prix. If you fancy a bit of Formula 1 action yourself, head to the jaw-droppingly huge **Ferrari World** (ⓦ ferrariworldabudhabi. com) theme park just down the road, offering a range of rides.

Cafés

Lebanon Flower

MAP P.92

Off 26th St ☏ 02 665 8700. Daily 8am–3am.
This enduringly popular restaurant is the best place in the city to fill up on inexpensive Middle Eastern food, with a well-prepared range of fish and meat grills, kebabs (45–60dh) and mezze.

Le Café

MAP P.92

Emirates Palace Hotel, Corniche Rd West ☏ 02 690 7999, ⓦ emiratespalace.com. Daily 6.30am–1am.
The *Emirates Palace*'s beautiful foyer café makes a memorable setting for one of the Middle East's most sumptuous afternoon teas; choose either traditional English or Arabian style (served 2–6pm; 260dh).

Restaurants

Finz

MAP P.92

Beach Rotana Hotel, 10th St, Tourist Club Area ☏ 02 697 9350, ⓦ rotana.com/beachrotana. Sun–Wed 7–11.30pm, Thurs–Fri 12.30–3.30pm & 7–11.30pm, Sat 12.30–4pm & 7–11.30pm.
One of the best seafood restaurants in town, occupying an unusual A-frame wooden dining room and terrace with superb views of Al Maryah Island. The menu features a wide selection of fish and seafood – ceviche, whole Maine crab, Mediterranean sea bass and so on. Mains from 140dh.

India Palace

MAP P.92

As Salam St, Tourist Club Area ☏ 02 644 8777, ⓦ indiapalace.ae. Daily noon–midnight.
Long-established and pleasantly old-fashioned Indian restaurant, serving up a big spread of tasty and very reasonably priced North Indian meat, seafood and veg offerings. Veg mains from 25dh, non-veg from 35dh.

Mezzaluna

MAP P.92

Emirates Palace Hotel, Corniche Rd West ☏ 02 690 7999, ⓦ emiratespalace.com. Daily 12.30–3pm & 7–11pm.
One of the more affordable of the *Emirates Palace*'s string of upmarket eating venues, serving traditional Italian and Mediterranean cuisine. Mains 90–215dh.

Stratos

MAP P.92

Le Royal Méridien hotel, Sheikh Khalifa St ☏ 800 101 101, ⓦ stratosabudhabi.com. Mon–Sat 7pm–2am.
Bird's-eye city views are the main attraction at this revolving lounge bar and restaurant. The modern European-style food's not bad either, comprising a mix of seafood starters and Josper-cooked meat mains (190–400dh). You can also just visit for a drink or a lavish afternoon tea (3–6pm, from around 230dh).

Bar

Brauhaus

MAP P.92

Beach Rotana Hotel, 10th St, Tourist Club Area ☏ 02 697 9000, ⓦ rotana.com/beachrotana. Sun–Thurs 3pm–1am, Fri–Sat noon–1am.
This convivial pub-cum-restaurant makes a surprisingly convincing stab at an authentic Bavarian *bierkeller*, with speciality German beers on tap or by the bottle and a good range of food to soak it all up with, served to the accompaniment of Bavarian marching bands and other Teutonic sounds. Very popular, so arrive early if you want to bag a seat.

ACCOMMODATION

Burj al Arab

Accommodation

Dubai has a vast range of accommodation, much of it aimed squarely at big spenders. At the top end of the market, the city has some of the most stunning hotels on the planet, from the futuristic *Burj al Arab* – the world's first "seven-star" hotel – to traditional Arabian-themed palaces such as *Al Qasr* and the *One&Only Royal Mirage*, and suave modern city hotels like *Raffles* and *Grosvenor House* – as well as the vast *Atlantis* mega-resort. There are plenty of mid-range options scattered across the city, too, although virtually all establishments in this price range tend towards the functional and characterless, providing comfortable lodgings but not much else. There's no real budget accommodation in Dubai, and you won't find a double room anywhere in the city for much less than about 300dh (US$80), or a single for much under 250dh (US$70). The good news is that stringent government regulations and inspections mean standards are reliable even at the cheapest hotels – all are scrupulously clean and fairly well maintained, and come with a/c, en-suite bathroom, plenty of hot water, satellite TV, fridge and wi-fi (usually, but not always, free).

Bur Dubai

ARABIAN COURTYARD MAP P.26, POCKET MAP M12. Al Fahidi St. Al Fahidi metro ☎ 04 351 9111, ⓦ arabiancourtyard. com. In a brilliantly central location opposite the Dubai Museum, this attractive four-star is a distinct cut above the other mid-range places in Bur Dubai – and usually excellent value too. Decor features a nice mix of modern and Arabian styles, while facilities include a small gym and spa – though the pool is tiny. **665dh**

BARJEEL HERITAGE GUEST HOUSE MAP P.26, POCKET MAP M10. Shindagha waterfront. Al Ghubaiba metro ☎ 04 393 8700, ⓦ barjeelguesthouse.com. Located between Al Ghubaiba metro station and Sheikh Saeed al Maktoum House, this appealing heritage guesthouse occupies a fine old historic building in a picture-perfect location on the Shindagha waterfront. Rooms are arranged around a beautiful internal courtyard and attractively furnished in traditional Arabian style, and there's also a good restaurant attached. **396dh**

FOUR POINTS SHERATON BUR DUBAI MAP P.26, POCKET MAP M13. Khalid Bin al Waleed Rd. Al Fahidi metro ☎ 04 397 7444, ⓦ fourpointsburdubai.com. Understated but very comfortable four-star with nicely furnished rooms in simple international style and good facilities including a gym, (smallish) swimming pool, the excellent *Antique Bazaar* restaurant and the cosy *Viceroy Bar* (see page 33). **385dh**

ORIENT GUEST HOUSE MAP P.26, POCKET MAP N12. Bastakiya. Al Fahidi metro ☎ 04 353 4448, ⓦ orientguesthouse.com. Cosy heritage hotel (albeit not quite as atmospheric as the nearby *XVA*), occupying an old Bastakiya house and offering eleven rooms attractively decorated with antique-style wooden furniture and four-poster beds. 362dh

TIME PALACE HOTEL MAP P.26, POCKET MAP M11. Just off Al Fahidi St. Al Ghubaiba metro ☎ 04 353 2111, ⓦ timepalacehotel. com. The most consistently reliable budget hotel in Bur Dubai, with spacious and very well-maintained rooms in an unbeatable location just up from the main entrance to the Textile Souk. Tends to get booked up well in advance, so reserve early. 300dh

XVA MAP P.26, POCKET MAP N12. Bastakiya. Al Fahidi metro ☎ 04 353 5383, ⓦ xvahotel.com. Atmospheric hotel and café (see page 32) tucked away around the back of a fine old Bastakiya house. Rooms are on the small side but brimming with character, featuring Arabian furnishings, slatted windows and four-poster beds, plus captivating views over the surrounding wind towers. Good value. 550dh

Deira

AHMEDIA HERITAGE GUEST HOUSE MAP P.36, POCKET MAP N11. Old Baladiya Rd. Al Ras metro ☎ 04 225 0085, ⓦ ahmediaguesthouse.com. Attractive

and competitively priced heritage hotel in a very central but peaceful location right next to Al Ahmadiya School, with fifteen rooms attractively done up with traditional wooden furniture and four-poster beds. 362dh

CROWNE PLAZA DUBAI DEIRA MAP P.36, POCKET MAP P4. Salahuddin Rd. Salah al Din metro ☎ 04 262 5555, ⓦ crowneplaza.com. One of Deira's oldest accommodation landmarks, formerly the *Renaissance Hotel*, now given a spruce modern makeover. The unfashionable address (although very handy for both airport and metro) and factory-like exterior don't immediately inspire, but the airy atrium and bigger-than-average rooms tick all the right boxes, while facilities include a health club, medium-sized pool, plus bar and a couple of restaurants. 326dh

HILTON DUBAI CREEK MAP P.36, POCKET MAP N4. Baniyas Rd. Al Rigga metro ☎ 04 227 1111, ⓦ hilton.com/dubai. Deira's smartest hotel, with chrome-clad public areas and stylish, well-equipped rooms decorated in minimalist whites and creams; most also have grand Creek views. There's also a health club, a small rooftop pool and the excellent *Table 9* restaurant (see page

Room rates

Hotels in all price ranges chop and change their room rates constantly according to the time of year and demand, so a hotel may be brilliant value one week, and a rip-off the next. The rates given in our reviews are only a very rough guide to average prices; actual costs may sometimes be significantly lower or higher, with price fluctuations of well over fifty percent at the same property quite common. Prices usually (but not always) depend on the **season**. In general, they're highest during the cool winter months from November to February (especially during the Dubai Shopping Festival), and cheapest in high summer (June to August), when rates at some places can tumble by thirty percent or more. **Taxes** (a ten percent service charge, a ten percent municipality tax and a tourism fee of 5–15dh per day depending on the star rating of the accommodation) are sometimes included in the quoted rate, but not always, so check when booking or you might find yourself suddenly having to cough up an extra twenty percent. All the prices given in these reviews are for the **cheapest double room in high season** (excluding Christmas and New Year), inclusive of all taxes.

40). **439dh**

HYATT PLACE AL RIGGA MAP P.36, POCKET MAP O4. Al Rigga Rd. Al Rigga metro ⓣ 04 608 1234, ⓦ dubaialrigga. place.hyatt.com. Similar to the *Hyatt Place* at Baniyas Square (see below), a bit further out, but close to the metro and all the amenities of lively Al Rigga Road. Super-spacious rooms feature smart decor, big picture windows and all the usual mod-cons, and there's also a restaurant, bar, and smallish outdoor pool. **468dh**

HYATT PLACE BANIYAS SQUARE MAP P.36, POCKET MAP O12. Baniyas Square. Baniyas Square metro ⓣ 04 404 1234, ⓦ dubaibaniyassquare.place.hyatt. com. Bringing a long overdue touch of 21st-century style to the dated hotels surrounding Baniyas Square, this brand new Hyatt offers quality but relatively affordable accommodation with five-star comforts but without all the trappings of a big hotel. The very spacious, almost loft-style rooms, come with huge floor-to-ceiling windows (and good views over the square from some), and cool decor, while facilities include a restaurant, coffee-lounge-cum-bar and a small pool. **595dh**

RADISSON BLU DUBAI DEIRA CREEK MAP P.36, POCKET MAP O13. Baniyas Rd. Union metro ⓣ 04 282 1111, ⓦ radissonblu.com. The oldest five-star in the city, this *grande dame* of a hotel still has plenty going for it: an extremely central location, a good spread of restaurants and a scenic position right on the Creek, of which all rooms have a view. Generally excellent value. **441dh**

SHERATON DUBAI CREEK MAP P.36, POCKET MAP N3. Baniyas Rd. Union metro ⓣ 04 228 1111, ⓦ sheraton.com/dubai. This old-fashioned five-star enjoys a scenic creekside setting and opulent public areas with lots of shiny white marble. Roughly half the rooms have Creek views (the higher the better) and facilities include a small pool plus good in-house restaurants, including the excellent *Ashiana* (see page 39) and *Vivaldi's*, while rates are very competitive. **545dh**

The inner suburbs

GRAND HYATT MAP P.44, POCKET MAP L7. Sheikh Rashid Rd, Oud Metha. Dubai Healthcare City metro ⓣ 04 317 1234, ⓦ dubai.grand.hyatt.com. This colossus of a hotel is grand in every sense – the vast atrium alone could easily swallow two or three smaller establishments, while facilities include four pools, spa, kids' club, gym, thirteen restaurants and bars, and beautiful, spacious grounds. The only real drawback is its middle-of-nowhere location, although it is conveniently close to the metro and major roads. **950dh**

PARK HYATT MAP P.44, POCKET MAP N6. Dubai Creek Golf and Yacht Club, Garhoud. Deira City Centre metro ⓣ 04 602 1234, ⓦ dubai.park.hyatt.com. Alluring five-star set in a beautiful complex of quasi-Moroccan-style buildings surrounded by extensive grounds with plenty of palm trees. Rooms (some with fine Creek views) are unusually large, while facilities include a big pool and the superb Amara spa, plus the *Thai Kitchen* (see page 49) restaurant and attractive marina-side Shisha Lounge. **1028dh**

RAFFLES MAP P.44, POCKET MAP L6. Sheikh Rashid Rd, Oud Metha. Dubai Healthcare City metro ⓣ 04 324 8888, ⓦ raffles.com/dubai. Vying with the *Park Hyatt* for the title of Dubai's finest city-centre hotel, the spectacular *Raffles* is designed in the form of an enormous postmodern pyramid, with a beautifully executed blend of Egyptian and Asian styling. Rooms feature silky-smooth contemporary decor and fine city views, while facilities include a good selection of eating and drinking establishments, a big pool and extensive grounds. **1045dh**

Sheikh Zayed Road and Downtown Dubai

ARMANI HOTEL MAP P.52, POCKET MAP E4. Floors 5–8 & 38–39, Burj Khalifa. Burj Khalifa/Dubai Mall metro ⓣ 04 888 3888, ⓦ armanihotels.com. Located in the iconic Burj Khalifa, this was the world's first Armani hotel when it opened in 2010.

The whole place is kitted out in furnishings from Giorgio's Casa Armani homeware range – all muted whites, greys, browns and blacks. Facilities include a string of fine eating and drinking venues (see page 56), a cool spa and pool. **3200dh**

DUSIT THANI MAP P.52, POCKET MAP F4. Sheikh Zayed Rd. Financial Centre metro ⓣ 04 343 3333, ⓦ dusit.com. Thai-owned and -styled five-star combining serene interior design and ultra-attentive service. Rooms are stylishly decorated in soothing creams and browns, while facilities include the excellent *Benjarong* restaurant (see page 56). **775dh**

IBIS WORLD TRADE CENTRE MAP P.52, POCKET MAP H4. Sheikh Zayed Rd. World Trade Centre metro ⓣ 04 332 4444, ⓦ accorhotels.com. The cheapest lodgings in this part of town. Rooms are small but comfortable (with nice views from higher ones), and guests can use the fitness centre and pools at the adjacent *Novotel* for a small fee. **255dh**

JUMEIRAH EMIRATES TOWERS MAP P.52, POCKET MAP G4. Sheikh Zayed Rd. Emirates Towers metro ⓣ 04 330 0000, ⓦ jumeirahemiratestowers. com. Occupying the smaller of the two iconic Emirates Towers, this exclusive establishment is generally rated the top business hotel in the city, catering mainly to senior execs on expense accounts. Rooms appear designed to calm the nerves of stressed-out CEOs, with muted colours and soothingly understated furnishings, and there's also a dedicated ladies' floor, plus a good-sized pool and health club. **900dh**

MANZIL DOWNTOWN DUBAI MAP P.52, POCKET MAP E5. Sheikh Mohammed bin Rashid Blvd (Emaar Blvd), Old Town. Burj Khalifa/Dubai Mall metro ⓣ 04 428 5888, ⓦ vida-hotels.com. Stylish little hotel with an attractive mix of contemporary and traditional Arabian styling. Rooms are on the small side, although there's a decent spread of amenities including a reasonable-sized pool and the pleasant *Nezesaussi* sports-themed pub-restaurant. The nearby *Vida Downtown Dubai* hotel (ⓣ 04 428

6888, ⓦ vida-hotels.com), run by the same company, is very similar. **1049dh**

RODA AL MUROOJ MAP P.52, POCKET MAP F4. Financial Centre Rd ⓣ 04 321 1111, ⓦ roda-hotels.com/al-murooj/; Financial Centre metro. In a handy location between Sheikh Zayed Rd and the Dubai Mall, this sprawling five-star feels more like a beachside resort than a city-centre hotel. Outside, the extensive, attractively landscaped gardens are dotted with lively restaurants and bars, including the ever-popular *Double Decker* pub (see page 58). Inside there's plenty of contemporary style, with spacious and attractively furnished rooms, very competitively priced. **807dh**

THE PALACE MAP P.52, POCKET MAP E5. Sheikh Mohammed bin Rashid Blvd (Emaar Blvd), Old Town. Burj Khalifa/Dubai Mall metro ⓣ 04 428 7888, ⓦ theaddress.com. Opulent, Arabian-themed "city-resort" with lavish, quasi-Moroccan styling and a perfect lakeside view of the Dubai Fountain and Burj, best enjoyed from the fine in-house *Thiptara* restaurant (see page 57). Facilities include a superb spa and large lakeside pool. **1899dh**

SHANGRI-LA MAP P.52, POCKET MAP F4. Sheikh Zayed Rd. Financial Centre metro ⓣ 04 343 8888, ⓦ shangri-la.com. The most stylish hotel on Sheikh Zayed Rd, the *Shangri-La* is pure contemporary class – a beguiling mix of Zen-chic and Scandinavian-cool. Rooms come with smooth pine finishes, beautiful artworks and mirrors everywhere, while leisure facilities include one of the biggest pools in this part of town plus several excellent restaurants, including the seductive *Hoi An* (see page 56). **900dh**

TOWERS ROTANA MAP P.52, POCKET MAP G3. Sheikh Zayed Rd. Financial Centre metro ⓣ 04 343 8000, ⓦ rotana.com. This shiny four-star is usually one of the cheapest Sheikh Zayed Rd options – a bit run-of-the-mill compared to other nearby places but with comfortable rooms and amenities including a couple of decent in-house restaurants and the ever-popular *Long's Bar* (see page 59). **1190dh**

Jumeirah

DUBAI MARINE BEACH RESORT MAP P.101, POCKET MAP H1. Jumeirah Rd, near Jumeirah Mosque ☏ 04 346 1111, ⓦ dxbmarine.com. This pocket-sized resort is the only five-star in Dubai where you can be on the beach but also within easy striking distance of the old city. The central location means that beach and grounds don't compare with places further south, although the resort scores highly for its lively collection of bars and restaurants, and turns into a bit of a party palace after dark. **690dh**

The Burj al Arab and around

BURJ AL ARAB MAP P.66, POCKET MAP K15. ☏ 04 301 7777, ⓦ burj-al-arab.com. A stay in this staggering hotel (see page 64) is the ultimate Dubaian luxury. The "seven-star" facilities include fabulous split-level deluxe suites (the lowest category of accommodation – there are no ordinary rooms here), arrival in a chauffeur-driven Rolls and your own butler, access to the superlative Assawan Spa, a handful of spectacular restaurants and bars, and a gorgeous stretch of beach. **5000dh**

DAR AL MASYAF MAP P.66, POCKET MAP J16. Madinat Jumeirah ☏ 04 366 8888, ⓦ madinatjumeirah.com. A more intimate and upmarket alternative to the Madinat Jumeirah's big two hotels, *Dar al Masyaf* consists of a chain of modest, low-rise private villas scattered around the edges of the Madinat complex within extensive, palm-studded gardens. Each villa contains a small number of rooms, sharing an exclusive pool and decorated in the deluxe Arabian manner of *Al Qasr* and *Mina A'Salam*, whose myriad facilities they share. **1600dh**

IBIS MALL OF THE EMIRATES MAP P.66, POCKET MAP J18. 2A St, near the Mall of the Emirates. Mall of the Emirates metro ☏ 04 382 3000, ⓦ ibis. accorhotels.com. This cheery little no-frills hotel is usually the best bargain in southern Dubai, with good-value rooms and a decent location on the south side of the Mall of the Emirates. **325dh**

JUMEIRAH BEACH HOTEL MAP P.66, POCKET MAP L15. Jumeirah Rd ☏ 04 348 0000, ⓦ jumeirahbeachhotel.com. Famous old Dubai landmark (see page 66), and still an excellent place to stay, with a vast range of facilities including over twenty restaurants, five pools, diving centre – plus jaw-dropping views of the adjacent Burj al Arab. It's particularly good for families, with the Sinbad kids' club, spacious grounds and a fine stretch of beach with plenty of watersports available; guests also get unlimited access to Wild Wadi next door. **1700dh**

MINA A'SALAM MAP P.66, POCKET MAP K15. Madinat Jumeirah ☏ 04 366 8888, ⓦ madinatjumeirah.com. Part of the stunning Madinat Jumeirah complex, *Mina A'Salam* ("Harbour of Peace") shares the Madinat's Orientalist styling, with beautifully furnished rooms featuring traditional Arabian wooden furniture and fabrics. Facilities include a nice-looking stretch of private beach, three pools plus the forty-odd restaurants, bars and myriad shops of the adjacent Madinat complex. **3750dh**

AL QASR MAP P.66, POCKET MAP K16. Madinat Jumeirah ☏ 04 366 8888, ⓦ madinatjumeirah.com. This extravagant Arabian-themed hotel looks like something out of a film set, from the opulent public areas to the swanky rooms with show-stopping views, sumptuous Oriental decor and pretty much every luxury and mod con you can imagine. There's also a huge pool and all the facilities of the Madinat Jumeirah on your doorstep. **4080dh**

The Palm Jumeirah and Dubai Marina

THE ADDRESS DUBAI MARINA MAP P.74, POCKET MAP B16. Dubai Marina. DAMAC Properties metro ☏ 04 436 7403, ⓦ theaddress.com. The best of the non-beachfront hotels in this part of town, right next to the Marina Mall and as smooth as you like, with outstanding service and soothing decor in muted creams and browns. Rooms come with all mod cons including Nespresso machine and iPad; those on higher floors have terrific views, and small balconies to enjoy them from. Facilities include a smart 24hr gym and a huge ovoid pool – the biggest in the Marina. **1500dh**

ATLANTIS POCKET MAP E10.
Palm Jumeirah ☏ 04 426 0000, ⓦ atlantisthepalm.com. This vast mega-resort (see page 73) is the exact opposite of tasteful, but can't be beaten when it comes to in-house attractions, including a water park, dolphinarium, celebrity-chef restaurants, kicking bars and clubs, luxurious spa and vast swathes of sand. There are also excellent kids' facilities, making it a good place for a (pricey) family holiday, with everything you need under one very large roof, while staying here also gets you free or discounted admission to the otherwise expensive on-site activities. It's not the most peaceful place in town, however, more suited to an up-tempo family holiday than a romantic break. **1003dh**

GROSVENOR HOUSE MAP P.74,
POCKET MAP C16. Al Sufouh Rd. DAMAC Properties metro ☏ 04 399 8888, ⓦ grosvenorhouse-dubai.com. One of Dubai's slickest hotels, set slightly away from the seafront in a pair of elegantly tapering skyscrapers. The entire hotel is a model of contemporary cool, from the suave public areas right through to the elegantly furnished rooms. Facilities include a pool, two excellent spas, and one of the city's best selections of restaurants and bars (see page 78), while guests also have free use of the beach and facilities at the nearby Le Royal Méridien. **949dh**

HILTON DUBAI JUMEIRAH RESORT MAP
P.74, POCKET MAP B15. This The Walk at Jumeirah Beach Residence. Jumeirah Beach Residence 1 tram station ☏ 04 399 1111, ⓦ hilton.com/dubai. The glitzy Hilton boasts lots of shiny metal and carries an air of cosmopolitan chic – more of a city-slicker's beach bolt-hole than family seaside resort. Rooms are bright and cheerfully decorated, although facilities are relatively limited compared to nearby places. Outside there's a medium-sized pool and lovely (though rather small) terraced gardens running down to the sea. **949dh**

JUMEIRAH ZABEEL SARAY MAP P.74,
POCKET MAP C13. West Crescent, Palm Jumeirah ☏ 04 453 0000, ⓦ jumeirah.com. Easily the most extravagant of the many hotels to have opened in Dubai in recent years: relatively understated from outside, but a riot of quirky opulence within. Public areas and rooms are designed in lavish quasi-Ottoman style, while the hotel's spectacular array of bars and restaurants ranges through a whole encyclopedia of styles – fake Rajasthani palace (see page 78), faux French chateau, burlesque music hall and Eskimo spaceship (see page 78) – all beautifully done, and good fun besides. Facilities include the vast Talisse Ottoman Spa and in-house cinema, while outside there are beautiful grounds, a gorgeous infinity pool and extensive beach (with kids' club). Rates vary wildly, but are often good value. **800dh**

LE MÉRIDIEN MINA SEYAHI MAP
P.74, POCKET MAP D15. Al Sufouh Rd. Mina Seyahi tram station ☏ 04 399 3333, ⓦ lemeridien-minaseyahi. com. This venerable old five-star isn't much to look at and is one of Dubai's most dated big hotels, although it scores highly for its superb grounds and big swathe of beach, where you'll also find the kicking Barasti beachside bar (see page 80). **1000dh**

LE ROYAL MÉRIDIEN BEACH RESORT
AND SPA MAP P.74, POCKET MAP C15. The Walk at Jumeirah Beach Residence. Jumeirah Beach Residence 1 tram station ☏ 04 399 5555, ⓦ leroyalmeridien-dubai. com. This large and slightly overblown five-star lacks the style of some other places along the beach although it compensates with its extensive grounds and beach, complete with three larger-than-average pools – excellent for families. Facilities include the ostentatious, Roman-themed Caracalla Spa, a smart gym, tennis and squash courts, a kids' club and a good number of restaurants, including the excellent Rhodes Twenty10 (see page 79). Often excellent value. **1079dh**

ONE&ONLY THE PALM MAP P.74,
POCKET MAP C14. West Crescent, Palm

Jumeirah ⓘ 04 440 1010, ⓦ thepalm. oneandonlyresorts.com. A haven of intimate, understated luxury amid the burgeoning mega-resorts sprouting up around the Palm in an ever-increasing string of bling, *One&Only The Palm* is small, peaceful and very civilized (apart from the fearsome price tag). The style is quasi-Moorish, with hints of the Alhambra in Granada, and neat gardens lining a gorgeous pool, and there's also a fine spa and almost 500m of private beach. A boat shuttle runs guests over to the mainland from the hotel's own marina, where you'll also find the attractive waterside *101* bar-restaurant (see page 80). 3230dh

ONE&ONLY ROYAL MIRAGE MAP P.74, POCKET MAP E15. Al Sufouh Rd. Media City/ Palm Jumeirah tram stations ⓘ 04 399 9999, ⓦ royalmirage.oneandonlyresorts. com. The most romantic hotel in town, this dreamy resort is the perfect *One Thousand and One Nights* fantasy made flesh, with a superb sequence of quasi-Moroccan-style buildings scattered amid extensive, palm-filled grounds. The whole complex is actually three hotels in one: *The Palace*, the *Arabian Court* and the *Residence & Spa*, each a little bit more sumptuous (and expensive) than the last. Rooms feature Arabian decor, reproduction antique wooden furniture and colourful rugs, while facilities include a 1km stretch of private beach, four pools, the delectable Oriental hammam-style spa and some of the best restaurants and bars in town (see page 78) – all at sometimes surprisingly affordable rates. 3600dh

RITZ-CARLTON MAP P.74, POCKET MAP B15. The Walk at Jumeirah Beach Residence. Jumeirah Beach Residence 1 tram station ⓘ 04 399 4000, ⓦ ritzcarlton.com. Set in a low-rise, Tuscan-style ochre building, this stylish establishment is one of the classiest in the city. Rooms are spacious, with slightly chintzy decor, while public areas boast all the charm of a luxurious old country house, especially in the sumptuous lobby lounge. There's also a big and very quiet stretch of private beach and gardens, an attractive spa and good kids' facilities. 1700dh

SHERATON JUMEIRAH BEACH MAP P.74, POCKET MAP A15. The Walk at Jumeirah Beach Residence. Jumeirah Beach Residence 2 tram station ⓘ 04 399 5533, ⓦ sheraton.com/jumeirahbeach. The area's most low-key five-star, particularly good for families, with extensive palm-studded gardens and beach and a watersports centre, while kids get their own pool area, playground and day-care club. Usually a bit cheaper than the nearby competition, although no bargain. 690dh

Out of the city

AL AIN ROTANA MAP P.88. 120th Street ⓘ 03 754 5111, ⓦ rotana.com/alainrotana. This long-running five-star is easily the best of the city's rather limited selection of hotels, and conveniently close to the city centre as well. Rooms are large and well appointed, and there are also spacious gardens complete with a pair of pools and a couple of good in-house restaurants, including the fun *Min Zaman* (see page 89). 399dh

BAB AL SHAMS DESERT RESORT AND SPA ⓘ 04 809 6498, ⓦ meydanhotels.com/ babalshams. Hidden out in the desert a 45min drive from the airport, this gorgeous resort occupies a wonderfully atmospheric replica Arabian fort, with desert camel- and horseriding or falconry displays the order of the day, rather than lounging on the beach. Rooms are decorated in traditional Gulf style, with rustic ochre walls and Bedouin-style fabrics, while facilities include a magnificent infinity pool and a good selection of restaurants. 2100dh

DESERT PALM inside front cover flAP. ⓘ 04 323 8888, ⓦ desertpalm.peraquum. com. On the edge of Dubai, around a 20min drive from the city centre, the *Desert Palm* is a pleasantly laidback suburban bolt-hole, surrounded by polo fields, with distant views of the skyscrapers along Sheikh Zayed Rd. Rooms are beautifully designed and equipped with fancy mod-cons, while facilities include the superb in-house Lime Spa. 732dh

AL MAHA DESERT RESORT AND SPA Dubai Desert Conservation Reserve,

Al Ain Rd ☎ 04 832 9900, Ⓦ al-maha. com. Some 60km from Dubai, this very exclusive, very expensive resort occupies a picture-perfect setting amid the pristine Dubai Desert Conservation Reserve (see page 89) – gazelles and rare Arabian oryx can often been seen wandering through the grounds. The resort is styled like a Bedouin encampment, with accommodation in tented suites featuring handcrafted furnishings and artefacts plus small private pools, and stunning views of the surrounding dunes. Activities include falconry, camel treks, horseriding, archery, 4WD desert drives and guided nature walks; or you can just relax in the resort's serene spa. Full board (including two desert activities per day) around **6032dh**

Abu Dhabi

BEACH ROTANA MAP P.92. 10th St, Al Zahiyah ☎ 02 697 9000, Ⓦ rotana.com/beachrotana. Smart modern resort-style hotel in the so-called Tourist Club Area, one of Abu Dhabi downtown's liveliest areas. Rooms are spacious and attractively styled, and there's a nice stretch of waterfront beach and gardens, plus an excellent spread of places to eat and drink. **750dh**

EMIRATES PALACE MAP P.92. Corniche Rd West ☎ 02 690 9000, Ⓦ emiratespalace. com. Abu Dhabi's landmark hotel (see page 90) is the favoured residence of visiting heads of state and assorted celebrities, with every luxury you could think of, including lots of swanky restaurants and a vast swathe of beach. Rates aren't always as crushingly expensive as you might expect – check the website for offers. **1500dh**

INTERCONTINENTAL MAP P.92. Al Bateen St, Al Bateen ☎ 02 666 6888, Ⓦ intercontinental.com. One of the oldest five-stars in Abu Dhabi, and still among the best, set in an attractive coastal location on the quiet southern side of the centre with views of the nearby Etihad Towers and *Emirates Palace* beyond. Renovations have kept rooms in tiptop condition, while the excellent facilities include a huge pool, well-equipped gym, one of the city's best selections of restaurants and bars, and a fine swathe of beautiful white sand. **1420dh**

JUMEIRAH AT ETIHAD TOWERS MAP P.92. Etihad Towers, Corniche Rd West ☎ 02 811 5555, Ⓦ bit.ly/Jumeirah_Etihad. Swanky hotel occupying one of the five futuristic skyscrapers of the landmark Etihad Towers development – a cutting-edge alternative to the staid *Emirates Palace* opposite. Rooms are large, luxurious and full of state-of-the-art mod cons, while facilities include three pools, private beach and a serene spa. **700dh**

ROYAL ROSE HOTEL MAP P.92. 1025 Sheikh Zayed the 1st St, Al Markaziyah ☎ 02 672 4000, Ⓦ royalrosehotel.com. The exterior of this luxurious hotel is a seventeenth-century French palace, both on the outside and inside there is just as much opulence and gold leaf as anywhere else in this city. **405dh**

SHANGRI-LA MAP P.92. Qaryat al Beri ☎ 02 509 8888, Ⓦ shangri-la.com/abudhabi. One of the city's most alluring hotels, with gorgeous Arabian Nights decor, huge gardens, four pools, the lovely Chi spa, a gorgeous infinity pool which appears to flow straight into the sea, and wonderful views of the Sheikh Zayed Mosque. **1000dh**

ESSENTIALS

Highway intersection and the Dubai Metro

Arrival

Unless you're travelling overland from neighbouring Oman or sailing in on a cruise ship, you'll arrive at Dubai's sparkling, modern international **airport** close to the old city centre – although a handful of flights land at the new Al Maktoum International Airport in the far south of the city.

The airport (enquiries ☎ 04 224 5555, ⟨w⟩ dubaiairports.ae) is very centrally located in the district of Garhoud, around 7km from the city centre. There are three passenger terminals: Terminal 1 is where most international flights arrive; Terminal 3 is where all Emirates airlines flights land; and Terminal 2 is used by smaller regional carriers. All three terminals have plenty of ATMs and currency exchange booths, although if you want to rent a car (see page 110), you'll have to head to Terminal 1.

Both Terminal 1 and Terminal 3 have dedicated **metro stations**, offering quick and inexpensive transport into the city (see below). Alternatively, there are plentiful **taxis** (although note that they charge a 20dh flag fare when picking up from the airport, rather than the usual 5dh) and various **buses** (see ⟨w⟩ dubai-bus.com), although these are only really useful if you're staying in Deira or Bur Dubai and know where you're going; note that (as for the metro) you'll have to buy a Nol card or ticket (see box) before boarding the bus.

Getting around

Dubai is very spread out – it's around 25km from the city centre down to Dubai Marina – but getting around is relatively straightforward and inexpensive, thanks mainly to the excellent metro system. Taxis are also plentiful, while there are also buses and boats, as well as cheap car rental. Full information about the city's public transport is available on the Roads & Transport Authority (RTA) website at ⟨w⟩ rta.ae. The RTA also provide an excellent **online travel planner**.

By metro

The **Dubai Metro** (⟨w⟩ rta.ae) offers a cheap, fast and convenient way of getting around, with state-of-the-art driverless trains and eye-catching modern stations. It consists of two lines: the 52km-long **Red Line**, running from Rashidiya, just south of the airport, down Sheikh Zayed Road to Jebel Ali; and the 22km-long **Green Line**, which arcs around the city centre, running from Al Qusais, north of the airport, via Deira and Bur Dubai and then down to the Creek at Jaddaf. **Trains** run roughly every 4–8 minutes, with services running Saturday to Thursday from around 5.30am to midnight (until 1am on Thurs), and on Fridays from 10am to 1am.

All trains have a dedicated carriage for **women and children** (look for the signs above the platform barriers) plus a **Gold Class** compartment at the front of/back of the train – these have slightly plusher seating and decor, although the main benefit is that they're usually fairly empty, meaning that you're pretty much guaranteed a seat, something you'll often struggle to find in ordinary carriages.

Fares are calculated according to the distance travelled, ranging from 3dh up to a maximum of 7.50dh for a single trip (or from 6dh to 15dh in Gold Class), or 20dh for an entire day's travel (40dh in Gold Class). **Children** under 5 or shorter than 0.9m travel free.

By tram

Opened in late 2014, the new **Dubai Tram** has plugged one of the last major holes in the city's transport infrastructure, offering a convenient (if not desperately fast) way of getting around the Marina and north towards Umm Suqeim – the system is eventually planned to extend all the way up to the Madinat Jumeirah. The tram links seamlessly with the metro (with interconnecting stations at Jumeirah Lakes Towers and DAMAC Properties) and also the **Palm Monorail** (see page 73). As on the metro, fares are covered by the Nol system (see box) and all trams have Gold Class and women-and-children-only carriages. Operating hours are Saturday to Thursday 6.30am–1am, Friday 9am–1am, with departures every 8min.

By taxi

Away from areas served by the metro and tram, the only way of getting around Dubai quickly is by **taxi**. There are usually plenty of cabs around at all times of day and night (except in Bur Dubai and Deira during the morning and evening rush hours and after dark). **Fares** are pretty good value: there's a minimum charge of 12dh per ride, with a basic flag fare of 5dh (or 8/12 if a taxi is booked by phone during regular/peak hours), plus 1.71dh per kilometre. The exception is for taxis picked up from the airport, where a 20dh flag fare is imposed; there's also a 20dh surcharge if you take a taxi into Sharjah. You'll also have to pay a 4dh surcharge if your taxi travels through one of Dubai's four tollgates. **Tips** aren't strictly necessary, though many taxi drivers will automatically keep the small change from fares unless you specifically ask for it back.

Taxis are run by a number of firms (Cars Taxi, Dubai Taxi and National Taxis are the largest). Taxis operated

---

Nol cards

Almost all Dubai's public transport services – **metro**, **buses** and **trams** (but not abras) – are covered by the **Nol** system (ⓦ nol.ae). To use any of these forms of transport you'll need to buy a prepaid Nol card or ticket ahead of travel; no tickets are sold on board metro trains, buses or trams. Cards can be **bought** and **topped up** at any metro station; at one of the machines located at 64 bus stops around the city; or at branches of Carrefour, Spinneys, Waitrose and Redha Al-Ansari Exchange.

There are three types of Nol card; all three are valid for five years and can store up to 500dh worth of credit. The **Silver Card** costs 25dh (including 19dh credit). The **Gold Card** (same price) is almost identical, but allows users to travel on Gold Class compartments on the metro (see page 108). The **Blue Card**, available only to UAE citizens and Dubai residents, costs 70dh (including 20dh credit). An alternative to the three cards is the **Red Ticket** (a paper ticket, rather than a card). This has been specifically designed for tourists, costs just 2dh and is valid for 90 days, although it has to be pre-paid with the correct fare for each journey and can only be recharged up to a maximum of ten times. The Red Ticket also allows you to purchase a useful one-day pass (20/40dh in regular/Gold class) valid for all transport citywide.

by all companies can be booked on
☎ 04 208 0808.

By abra

Despite contemporary Dubai's
obsession with modern technology,
getting from one side of the Creek to
the other in the city centre is still a
charmingly old-fashioned experience,
involving a trip in one of the hundreds
of rickety little boats – or **abras** –
which ferry passengers between Deira
and Bur Dubai.

There are two main abra **routes**:
from Deira Old Souk Abra Station to
Bur Dubai Abra Station, and from Al
Sabkha Abra Station to Bur Dubai
Old Souk Abra Station. The **fare** is
just 1dh. Boats leave as soon as full
(meaning, in practice, every couple
of minutes), and the crossing takes
about five minutes. Abras run from
6am to midnight, and 24hr on the
route from Bur Dubai Old Souk to
Al Sabkha.

By ferry

Further memorable views of Dubai
from the water can be had by taking a
ride on the smart, modern Dubai Ferry.
Services run three times daily between
Bur Dubai and Dubai Marina (75min),
and once-daily from the Marina
towards the Burj al Arab via Palm
Jumeirah, and from Bur Dubai up the
Creek. Fares on all trips are 50dh.

By bus

Dubai has a well-developed and
efficient network of bus services,
though it's mainly designed around the
needs of low-paid expat workers so is
of only limited use for tourists – most
routes cover parts of the city that
casual visitors are unlikely to want

to reach. Most services originate or
terminate at either the **Gold Souk Bus
Station** in Deira or **Al Ghubaiba Bus
Station** in Bur Dubai (many services
call at both). Stops elsewhere are
clearly signed. Buses are included
in the **Nol ticket scheme**, meaning
that you'll need to be in possession
of a paid-up Nol card or ticket (see
page 109) before you get on the bus;
tickets aren't sold on board.

Buses to **Sharjah** leave from Al
Ghubaiba Bus Station, and also from
Al Sabkha Bus Station in the middle of
Deira (24hr; departures roughly every
20min from each station; 45min–1hr;
10dh). Buses to **Abu Dhabi** leave from
Al Ghubaiba (5am–11.30pm every
20min; 2hr–2hr 30min; 30dh) and from
Ibn Battuta metro station (Fri hourly
from 5am to noon, then every 30–40min
until 11pm; Sat–Thurs every 30min
from 5am to 10pm; 1hr 30min–2hr;
30dh). Minibuses to **Al Ain** leave from
Al Ghubaiba (every 40min from 5.40pm
to 10pm; 20dh). Nol cards can be used
on some Sharjah and Abu Dhabi buses
(but not on Al Ain services), or just buy
a ticket at the bus station.

By car

Renting a car is another option, but
comes with a couple of caveats.
Driving in Dubai isn't for the
faint-hearted: the city's roads are
permanently busy and standards
of driving wayward. **Navigational
difficulties** are another big problem,
given the city's ever-evolving layout.

For **car rental** contact any of
the following: Avis (🖮avisuae.
ae); Budget (🖮budget-uae.com);
Europcar (🖮europcardubai.com); Hertz
(🖮hertz.ae); Sixt (🖮sixt.ae); Thrifty
(🖮thriftyuae.com).

Tours

Dubai has dozens of identikit tour
operators who pull in a regular supply

of punters in search of the instant
"Arabian" experience. The emphasis is

Tour operators

Alpha Tours ⓣ 04 294 9888, ⓦ alphatoursdubai.com
Arabian Adventures ⓣ 04 303 4888, ⓦ arabian-adventures.com
Dubai Private Tour ⓣ 04 396 1444, ⓦ dubaiprivatetour.com
Funtours ⓣ 04 283 0889, ⓦ funtoursdubai.com
Knight Tours ⓣ 04 343 7725, ⓦ knighttours. ae
Lama Tours ⓣ 04 297 3993, ⓦ lamadubai.com
Orient Tours ⓣ 04 282 8238, ⓦ orienttours.ae
Platinum Heritage Luxury Tours ⓣ 04 388 4044, ⓦ platinum-heritage.com
Travco ⓣ 04 336 6643, ⓦ travcotravel.ae

firmly on stereotypical **desert safaris** and touristy dhow **dinner cruises**, although a few operators offer more unusual activities ranging from falconry displays to helicopter rides. **Prices** can vary quite considerably from operator to operator, so it's worth shopping around, although you generally get what you pay for, and some of the cheaper operators cut more corners than you might be comfortable with.

City tours

Generic city tours are offered by all our recommended general tour operators (see box), but for more original insights you might contact the **Sheikh Mohammed Centre for Cultural Understanding** in Bastakiya (ⓣ 04 353 6666, ⓦ cultures.ae) which runs interesting tours of Jumeirah Mosque and Bastakiya, along with other cultural events (see page 27). **Wonder Bus Tours** (ⓦ wonderbusdubai.net) also run innovative city tours, aboard the bizarre-looking Wonder Bus – half bus and half boat – starting off by road and then taking to the Creek. Trips last about one hour and cost 150–170dh (105–120dh for children aged 3–11).

If you've got the cash you might consider an airborne tour of the city, offering peerless views of the Creek and coast. **Seaplane** tours are offered by Seawings (ⓦ seawings.ae), while **helicopter** rides around the city can be arranged by several of the operators listed below, including Arabian Adventures, starting from around 1000dh per person for a 20min flight.

Boat cruises

A more leisurely alternative to the standard Creek crossing by abra is to **charter your own boat** (120dh/hr per boat). Starting from the city centre, in an hour you can probably get down to the Dubai Creek Golf Club and back. To find an abra for rent, head to the nearest abra station and ask around.

Alternatively you could go on one of the ever-popular after-dark Creek **dinner cruises**, which can be booked through any tour operator, as well as many of the city's hotels. Most of these use traditional old wooden dhows, offering the chance to wine and dine on the water as your boat sails sedately up and down the Creek. A number of operators now also offer similar dinner cruises sailing between skyscrapers at Dubai Marina. Standard cruises last two hours and cost anything from around 150dh up to 400dh, inclusive of a buffet dinner and onboard entertainment.

Classy cruises, using a state-of-the-art, modern boat, are run by **Bateaux Dubai** (ⓣ 04 814 5553, ⓦ bateauxdubai.com; 415dh); cheaper but reliable operators include **Al**

Mansour Dhow (☏ 04 222 7171; 235dh) and **Rikks Cruises** (☏ 04 458 6664, ✆ rikks.net; around 175dh).

Desert safaris

One thing that virtually every visitor to Dubai does at some point is go on a **safari** to see some of the desert scenery surrounding Dubai. Although virtually all tours put the emphasis firmly on cheap thrills and touristy gimmicks, most people find the experience enjoyable, in a rather cheesy sort of way.

The vast majority of visitors opt for one of the endlessly popular **half-day safaris** (also known as "sunset safaris"). These are offered by every tour operator, and though the cost ranges from around 175dh up to 375dh – the more expensive tours generally offering superior service, better-quality food and a wider range of entertainment – the basic ingredients remain the same. Tours are in large 4WDs holding around eight passengers. You'll be picked up from your hotel between 3 and 4pm and then driven out into the desert. The usual destination is an area 45 minutes' drive out of town, opposite the massive dune popularly known as Big Red where you'll enjoy a spot of **dune-bashing** – driving at high speed up and down increasingly precipitous dunes amid great sprays of sand. You might also be given the chance to try your hand at a brief bit of **sand-skiing**. As dusk falls, you'll be driven off to one of the dozens of optimistically named desert "Bedouin camps" where attractions will typically include (very short) camel rides, henna painting, dressing up in Gulf national costume, and having your photo taken with an Emirati falcon perched on your arm. A passable international buffet dinner is then served, after which a belly dancer performs for another half-hour or so. The whole thing winds up at around 9.30pm, after which you'll be driven back to Dubai.

Directory

Crime and drugs

Dubai is an exceptionally safe city – although a surprising number of tourists and expats manage to get themselves arrested for various breaches of local law. Violent crime is virtually unknown, and even instances of petty theft, pickpocketing and the like are relatively uncommon. The only time you're ever likely to be at risk is while driving. If you need to **call the police** in an emergency, dial ☏ 999. You can also contact the police's 24hr Tourist Security Department toll-free on ☏ 800 423 if you have an enquiry or complaint which you think they could help you with.

You should not on any account attempt to enter (or even transit through) Dubai while in possession of any form of **illegal substance**. The death penalty is imposed for drug trafficking, and there's a mandatory four-year sentence for anyone caught in possession of drugs or other proscribed substances. It's vital to note that this doesn't just mean carrying drugs in a conventional sense, but also includes having an illegal substance in your **bloodstream or urine**, or being found in possession of even **microscopic amounts** of a banned substance, even if invisible to the naked eye. Note that poppy seeds (even in bakery products) are also banned. Dubai's hardline anti-drugs regime also extends to certain **prescription drugs**, including codeine and melatonin, which are also treated as illegal substances. If you're on any form of prescription medicine you're supposed to bring a doctor's letter and the original prescription from home, and to bring no more than three months' supply into the UAE.

Culture and etiquette

Despite its glossy Western veneer and apparently liberal ways, it's important to remember that Dubai is an Islamic state, and that visitors are expected to comply with local cultural norms or risk the consequences.

There are a few simple rules to remember if you want to stay out of trouble. During **Ramadan** remember that between dawn and dusk eating, drinking, smoking or chewing gum in public are a definite no-no, as are singing, dancing and swearing in public (you are, however, free to eat and drink in any of the carefully screened-off dining areas set up in hotels throughout the city, while alcohol is also served discreetly after dark in some places). At any time, public displays of **drunkenness** contravene local law, and could get you locked up. Driving while under any sort of influence is even more of a no-no. Inappropriate public behaviour with members of the opposite sex can result in, at best, embarrassment, or, at worst, a spell in prison. Holding hands or a peck on the cheek is probably just about OK, but any more passionate **displays of affection** are severely frowned upon. **Offensive gestures** are another source of possible danger. Giving someone the finger or even just sticking out your tongue might be considered rude at home but can get you jailed in Dubai.

In terms of general etiquette, except around the hotel pool, **modest dress** is expected of all visitors. Dressing "indecently" is potentially punishable under law (even if actual arrests are extremely rare), although exactly what constitutes indecent attire isn't clearly defined. If you're fortunate enough to spend any time with Emiratis, remember that only the right hand should be used for eating and drinking (this rule also applies in Indian establishments), and don't offer to shake the hand of an Emirati woman unless she extends hers toward you.

Electricity

UK-style **sockets** with three square pins are the norm (although you might occasionally encounter Indian-style round-pin sockets in budget hotels in Bur Dubai and Deira). The city's **current** runs at 220–240 volts AC, meaning that UK appliances will work directly off the mains supply, although US appliances will probably require a transformer.

Embassies and consulates

Foreign embassies are mainly located in the UAE's capital, Abu Dhabi, although many countries also maintain consulates in Dubai.

Australia Consulate-General, Level 25, BurJuman Business Tower, Khalifa bin Zayed Rd, Bur Dubai ☏ 04 508 7100, ⓦ uae.embassy.gov.au.

Canada Consulate-General, 19th Floor, Emirates Towers (Business Tower), Sheikh Zayed Rd ☏ 04 404 8444, ⓦ canadainternational.gc.ca.

Ireland Embassy, Al Yasat Street (off 6th Street), Al Bateen, Abu Dhabi ☏ 02 495 8200, ⓦ embassyofireland.

New Zealand Embassy, Office 6A, Level 6, Emirates Tower, Sheikh Zayed Road ☏ 04 270 0100, ⓦ mfat.govt.nz.

South Africa Consulate-General, 3rd Floor, New Sharaf Building, Khaleed bin al Waleed St, Bur Dubai ☏ 04 397 5222, ⓦ dirco.gov.za/dubai.

UK Embassy, Al Seef Rd, Bur Dubai ☏ 04 309 4444, ⓦ ukinuae.fco.gov.uk/en.

US Consulate-General, Corner of Al Seef and Sheikh Khalifa bin Zayed roads, Bur Dubai ☏ 04 309 4000, ⓦ dubai.usconsulate.gov.

LGBTQ travellers

Dubai is one of the world's less LGBTQ-friendly destinations. Homosexuality is illegal under UAE law, with punishments of up to ten years in prison – a useful summary of the present legal situation and recent prosecutions can be found at ⓦen. wikipedia.org/wiki/LGBT_rights_in_ the_United_Arab_Emirates. Despite this, a very clandestine gay scene exists, attracting both foreigners and Arabs from even less permissive cities around the Gulf, although gay parties in Dubai are usually only publicised via social media and word of mouth. Relevant websites are routinely censored within the UAE, so you'll probably have to do your online research before you arrive. A useful resources is ⓦequaldex.com/region/ united-arab-emirates.

Health

There are virtually no serious **health risks** in Dubai (unless you include the traffic). The city is well equipped with modern hospitals, while all four- and five-star hotels have English-speaking **doctors** on call 24hr. **Tap water** is safe to drink, while even the city's cheapest curry houses and shwarma cafés maintain good standards of **food hygiene**. The only genuine health concern is the **heat**. Summer temperatures regularly climb into the mid-forties, making sunburn, heatstroke and acute dehydration a real possibility, especially if combined with excessive alcohol consumption. Stay in the shade, and drink lots of water.

Pharmacies can be found all over the city, including a number run by the BinSina chain which are open 24hr (there's a list at ⓦdha.gov.ae). There are two main **government hospitals** with emergency departments: Dubai Hospital, between the Corniche and Baraha Street, Deira (ⓣ04 219 5000);

and Rashid Hospital, off Oud Metha Road, near Maktoum Bridge, Oud Metha (ⓣ04 219 2000). You'll need to pay for treatment, though cost should be recoverable through your travel insurance. **Private hospitals** with emergency departments include the American Hospital, off Oud Metha Road (opposite the *Mövenpick* hotel), Oud Metha (ⓣ04 337 5000, ⓦahdubai. com), and Emirates Hospital, opposite Jumeirah Beach Park, Jumeirah Beach Road, Jumeirah (ⓣ04 349 6666, ⓦemirateshospital.ae).

Internet

Wi-fi is available in pretty much every hotel in the city, usually in rooms. It's generally free although some places charge for it – often at extortionate rates. Check before you book. The city has frustratingly few **internet cafés**. The best area to look is Bur Dubai, which boasts a scattering of small places – try Aimei internet café (daily 8am–midnight; 5dh/hr) on 13c Sikka, behind the *Time Palace* hotel, or Futurespeed (daily 8am–11pm; 10dh/ hr) in the BurJuman centre (by the *Dôme* café). There are also various wi-fi hotspots around the city operated by the city's two telecom companies, Etisalat (ⓦetisalat.ae) and Du (ⓦdu. ae). Wi-fi is also available on the metro (10dh/hr), and for free in most coffee shops and restaurants.

Internet access in Dubai is subject to a certain modest amount of **censorship** including a blanket ban on anything remotely pornographic, plus gambling and dating sites, and pages which are considered religiously or culturally offensive.

Lost property

For major items of lost property, try asking at the nearest local police station. If you accidentally leave something in a taxi, call the RTA Contact Centre on ⓣ800 9090.

Emergency numbers

Ambulance ☎ 999
Fire ☎ 997
Police ☎ 999

Money

The UAE's currency is the **dirham** (abbreviated "dh" or "AED"), subdivided into 100 fils. The dirham is pegged against the US dollar at the rate of US$1=3.6725dh; other **exchange rates** at the time of writing were £1=5.5dh, €1=4dh. **Notes** come in 5dh, 10dh, 20dh, 50dh, 100dh, 200dh, 500dh and 1000dh denominations; there are also 2dh, 1dh, 50 fils and 25 fils coins.

There are plenty of **ATMs** all over the city which accept foreign Visa and MasterCards. All the big shopping malls have at least a few ATMs, as do some large hotels and almost all banks. All will also change **foreign cash**, and there are also plenty of **moneychangers**, including the reputable Al Ansari Exchange, which has branches all over the city (see ⓦ alansariexchange.com/en/branches).

Opening hours

Dubai runs on an Islamic rather than a Western schedule, meaning that the city operates according to a basic **five-day working week** running Sunday to Thursday, with Friday as the Islamic holy day. When people talk about the **weekend** in Dubai they mean Friday and Saturday. The most important fact to note is that many tourist sites and the Dubai Metro are **closed on Friday morning**, while **banks** usually open Saturday to Wednesday 8am–1pm and Thursday 8am–noon (some also reopen in the afternoon from 4.30–6.30pm). **Shops** in **malls** generally open daily from 10am to 10pm, and until midnight on Friday and Saturday (and sometimes Thursday as well); shops in **souks** follow a similar pattern, though many places close for a siesta between around 1pm and 4pm depending on the whim of the owner. Most **restaurants** open daily for lunch and dinner (although some more upmarket hotel restaurants open for dinner only). **Pubs** tend to open daily from around noon until 2am; **bars** from around 6pm until 2/3am.

Phones

The **country code** for the UAE is ☎ 971. The **city code** for Dubai is ☎ 04; Abu Dhabi is ☎ 02; Sharjah is ☎ 06; Al Ain is ☎ 03. To **call abroad from the UAE**, dial ☎ 00, followed by your country code and the number itself (minus its initial zero). To call Dubai from abroad, dial your international access code, then ☎ 9714, followed by the local subscriber number (minus the ☎ 04 city code). For **directory enquiries** call ☎ 181 (Etisalat) or ☎ 199 (Du).

Post

The two most convenient **post offices** for visitors are the Al Musalla Post Office (Sat–Thurs 7.30am–3pm) at Al Fahidi Roundabout, opposite the *Arabian Tea House Café* in Bur Dubai; and the Deira Post Office on Al Sabkha Road (Sat–Thurs 8am–8pm), near the intersection with Baniyas Road. Airmail letters to Europe, the US and Australia cost 5dh (postcards 3.50dh).

Smoking

Smoking is banned in Dubai in the vast majority of indoor public places, including offices, malls, cafés and restaurants (although it's permitted at most – but not all – outdoor venues, and in bars and pubs). Many **hotels** now provide nonsmoking rooms or nonsmoking floors – and a few places have banned smoking completely. During Ramadan, never smoke in public places in daylight hours.

Time

Dubai (and the rest of the UAE) runs on **Gulf Standard Time**. This is 4hr ahead of GMT, 3hr ahead of BST, 9hr ahead of North American Eastern Standard Time, 12hr ahead of North American Western Standard Time, 6hr behind Australian Eastern Standard Time, and 8hr behind New Zealand Standard Time. There is no daylight saving time in Dubai.

Tipping and taxes

Room rates at most of the city's more expensive hotels are subject to a ten percent **service charge** and an additional ten percent **government tax**; these taxes are sometimes included in quoted prices, and sometimes not. Check beforehand, or you may find your bill has suddenly inflated by twenty percent. The prices in most restaurants automatically include all relevant taxes and a ten percent service charge (though this isn't necessarily passed on to the waiters themselves); whether you wish to leave an additional **tip** is entirely your decision.

Tourist information

There's a frustrating lack of on-the-ground visitor information in Dubai – and not a single proper tourist office anywhere in the city. Online, the official government website (⊛ visitdubai. com) is worth a browse, although the best resource is the lively *Time Out*

Dubai, whether in magazine form – it's published weekly and available at bookshops all over the city – or online (⊛ timeoutdubai.com). It carries comprehensive listings about pretty much everything going on in Dubai, and is particularly good for information about the constantly changing nightlife scene, including club, restaurant and bar promotions and new openings.

Travellers with disabilities

Dubai is probably the Middle East's most accessible destination. Most of the city's modern **hotels** now make at least some provision for guests with impaired mobility, and many of the city's four- and five-stars now have specially adapted rooms. Quite a few of the city's **malls** also have special facilities, including disabled parking spaces and specially equipped toilets. Inevitably, most of the city's older heritage buildings are not accessible (although the Dubai Museum is).

Transportation is fairly well set up. The **Dubai Metro** incorporates facilities to assist visually and mobility-impaired visitors, including tactile guide paths, lifts and ramps, as well as wheelchair spaces in all compartments, while **accessible taxis** can be booked on ☎ 04 208 0808 (but best to give a couple of hours' notice) equipped with ramps and lifts. There are also dedicated facilities at the **airport**.

Travelling with children

Dubai has a vast array of attractions for children, although many come with hefty price tags attached. Most of the city's beach hotels have their own in-house **kids' clubs**, providing free childcare (usually catering for ages 4–12), while most larger shopping malls have dedicated kids' play areas. Most hotels can arrange **babysitting** services for a fee. Attractions designed especially for kids include:

Children's City Creek Park, Oud Metha (☎ 04 334 0808, ⓦ childrencity.ae; Dubai Healthcare City metro). Occupying an eye-catching series of brightly coloured red and blue buildings in Creek Park, Children's City is aimed at kids aged 2–15, with a subtle educational slant and various galleries with fun interactive exhibits and lots of touchscreens covering subjects including physical science, nature, international culture and space exploration. 15dh; children 3–15 years 10dh; under-2s free; family ticket for 2 adults and 2 children 40dh; 5dh park entry fee. Sun–Thurs 9am–7pm, Fri & Sat 2–8pm.

Dubai Dolphinarium Creek Park (just inside the park near Gate #1), Oud Metha (☎ 04 336 9773, ⓦ dubaidolphinarium.ae; Dubai Healthcare City metro). Three-daily shows (Mon–Sat at 11am, 2pm & 6pm; also Fri & Sat at 11pm; adults 105dh, children 50dh) with bottlenose dolphins and seals. Note that keeping dolpins in captivity is considered cruel.

Ferrari World Yas Island, Abu Dhabi (☎ 02 496 8000, ⓦ ferrariworldabudhabi.com). The blockbuster attraction at Abu Dhabi's Yas Island (see page 94), the "world's biggest indoor theme park" offers a wide range of Ferrari-themed rides and displays which will appeal both to kids and grown-ups. Adults and children over 1.3m 295dh; under 1.3m 230dh; under-3s free. Daily 11am–8pm.

KidZania Second floor, Dubai Mall (ⓦ kidzania.ae; Burj Khalifa/Dubai Mall metro). Innovative edutainment attraction based on an imaginary city where the kids are in charge. Children get the chance to dress up and role-play from 75 different grown-up professions and even earn their own money en route. Ages 17+ 75dh; ages 4–16 from 185dh; ages 2–3 105dh; under-2s free. Daily Sun–Wed 10am–10pm, Thurs till 11, Fri & Sat 9am–11pm.

Penguin Encounter Ski Dubai. Mall of the Emirates ☎ 800 386, ⓦ skidxb. com. Get up close to some of Ski Dubai's resident Gentoo and King penguins in these 40min "interactive penguin encounters". Encounters include close-up underwater viewing and the chance to interact with at least two of the little critters at close quarters.Warm clothing and gloves provided. 230dh. Daily noon–9pm.

Adventure Zone Yas Mall, Yas Island, Abu Dhabi (☎ 02 565 0996, ⓦ adventurehq.ae). 30min session 70dh, 60min 110dh, 90min 140dh. If the heat of Dubai does nothing to slow you or your kids down, try this place to spend a little energy. Try a climbing wall, a rope park or a trampoline park. Indoor caving could be a lot of fun too, and you can always opt for the classic, a football pitch. Sat–Wed 10am–10pm, Thurs-Fri 10am–midnight.

Festivals and events

Dubai hosts a number of world-class annual festivals showcasing film, music and the visual arts, while neighbouring Abu Dhabi also stages a number of leading cultural and sporting events. For a complete listing of events in the city, see ⓦ dubaicalendar.ae.

Traditional dhow racing

Jan ⓦ dimc.ae.
Traditional wooden dhows under sail at the Dubai International Marine Club in Dubai Marina.

Dubai Marathon

Mid-Jan ⓦ **dubaimarathon.org.**
Top distance runners battle it out.

Dubai Shopping Festival

One month in Jan/Feb
Shops citywide offer all sorts of sales bargains, with discounts of up to 75 percent, while the big malls lay on entertainment and children's events.

Dubai International Jazz Festival

Three days in Feb ⓦ **dubaijazzfest. com.**
Top local and international jazz and pop acts perform at Dubai Media City Amphitheatre.

Dubai Desert Classic

Four days in Feb
ⓦ **dubaidesertclassic.com.**
Major event on the PGA European Tour held at the Emirates Golf Club and attracting leading stars.

Dubai Tennis Championships

Two weeks in late Feb/early March
Established fixture on the international tennis calendar at the Dubai Tennis Stadium in Garhoud, pulling in top male and female players.

Art Dubai

Four days in mid-March ⓦ **artdubai. ae.**
Some 75 galleries from around the world exhibit at Madinat Jumeirah.

Dubai World Cup

March ⓦ **dubaiworldcup.com.**
The world's richest horse race, with a massive US$10 million in prize money, held at Meydan Racecourse.

Taste of Dubai

Three days in mid-March
ⓦ **tasteofdubaifestival.com.**
Live cookery exhibitions at Dubai Media City by local and visiting international celebrity chefs.

Abu Dhabi Desert Challenge

One week in March/April
ⓦ **abudhabidesertchallenge.com.**

Public holidays

There are nine public holidays in Dubai: three have fixed dates, while the other five shift annually according to the Islamic calendar (falling around 11 days earlier from year to year).
New Year's Day Jan 1.
Milad un Nabi (Birth of the Prophet Mohammed) Estimated dates: Oct 29, 2020; Oct 19, 2021; Oct 8, 2022; Sept 27, 2023.
Leilat al Meiraj (Ascent of the Prophet) Estimated dates: March 22, 2020; March 11, 2021; March 1, 2022;
Eid ul Fitr (the end of Ramadan; see above) Estimated dates: May 24, 2020; May 13, 2021; May 5, 2022; April 24, 2023.
Arafat (Haj) Day Estimated dates: July 30, 2020; July 19, 2021; July 9, 2022; June 28, 2023.
Eid al Adha (the Festival of the Sacrifice; see above) Estimated dates: July 31, 2020; July 20, 2021; July 10, 2022; June 29, 2023.**Al Hijra (Islamic New Year)** Estimated dates: Aug 21, 2020; Aug 10, 2021; July 30, 2022; July 19, 2023.
Martyrs' Day Nov 30.
National Day (see page 119) Dec 2.

Rally drivers, bikers and quad–bikers race each other across the desert.

Dubai Summer Surprises

Mid-June to mid-July
Mainly mall-based event with shopping bargains on offer and lots of live children's entertainment.

Ramadan

Estimated dates: April 23-May 23, 2020, April 13-May 12, 2021, April 3-May 2, 2022.
The Islamic holy month of Ramadan is observed with great care in Dubai. Muslims are required to fast from dawn to dusk, and as a tourist you are expected publicly to observe these strictures (see page 113). Fasting ends at dusk, at which point the city springs to life in a celebratory round of eating, drinking and socializing known as Iftar ("The Breaking of the Fast"). The atmosphere is particularly exuberant during Eid ul Fitr, the day marking the end of Ramadan, which erupts in an explosion of festivity. Precise dates for Ramadan vary according to local astronomical sightings of the moon.

Eid al Adha

Estimated dates: Aug 12, 2019; July 31, 2020; July 20, 2021.
Falling approximately 70 days after the end of Ramadan, the "Festival of the Sacrifice" celebrates the willingness of Ibrahim to sacrifice his son Ismail at the command of God.

Abu Dhabi F1 Grand Prix

Three days in Nov
Ⓦ **yasmarinacircuit.com.**
The Gulf's premier sporting event, held annually at the spectacular Yas Marina Circuit.

Dubai World Tour Championship

Four days in Nov Ⓦ **facebook.com/ DPWorldTourChampionship.**
Held at the Earth course, Jumeirah Golf Estates, this is the showpiece finale of the European Tour's season-long "Race to Dubai".

Dubai Rugby Sevens

Three days in late Nov/early Dec
Ⓦ **dubairugby7s.com.**
Annual IRB Sevens World Series tournament at Dubai's Sevens stadium, accompanied by some of the city's most raucous partying.

Dubai International Film Festival

One week in mid-Dec
Ⓦ **dubaifilmfest.com.**
International art-house films, with a particular focus on home-grown work and usually a few well-known celebs in attendance.

National Day

Dec 2
Independence day is celebrated with a raft of citywide events.

Chronology

c.5000 BC Earliest human settlement in the southern Gulf.

500–600 AD The UAE region becomes part of an extensive trade network dominated by the Sassanian (Iranian) empire; settlement of Jumeirah area.

c.630 Arrival of Islam.

751 and onwards The southern Gulf experiences a major boom in maritime trade following the shifting of the Islamic caliphate from Damascus to Baghdad.

1580 First European reference to Dubai, by the Venetian pearl merchant Gaspero Balbi.

1820 Britain signs series of treaties (or "truces") with various Gulf rulers, whose territories are henceforth known as the Trucial States.

1833 Around a thousand Bani Yas tribesmen from Abu Dhabi take control of Dubai under the leadership of Maktoum bin Buti.

1835 Britain formally recognizes Dubai and enters into treaty with it.

1841 Settlement of Deira begins. Over the next decade the town grows rapidly, attracting a cosmopolitan population of Arabs, Iranians, Indians and Pakistanis.

1894 Dubai declared a free port by Sheikh Maktoum bin Hasher. Iranian merchants begin arriving in the city.

1929 onwards Gradual collapse of the pearl trade following the Great Depression and Japanese discovery of artificial pearl culturing.

1958 Death of Sheikh Saeed, succeeded by his son Sheikh Rashid.

1960 Dubai International Airport is opened.

1960–61 The Creek is dredged, establishing Dubai as the southern Gulf's major port.

1963 The first bridge across the Creek – Maktoum Bridge – is opened.

1966 Oil is discovered in the offshore Fateh field.

1971 The British withdraw from the Trucial States, which are re-formed as the United Arab Emirates. Opening of Port Rashid.

1970s and 1980s Oil revenues are used to diversify Dubai's industrial base and create massive new infrastructure projects, such as Jebel Ali Port and Free Zone (1983), and the World Trade Centre (1979).

1990 Death of Sheikh Rashid; Sheikh Maktoum becomes ruler of Dubai, though Crown Prince Sheikh Mohammed also exerts increasing influence over the city's development.

1996 Dubai Shopping Festival held for the first time.

1998 Opening of the Burj al Arab.

2006 Death of Sheikh Maktoum; Sheikh Mohammed becomes ruler.

2008 Credit crunch hits Dubai; emirate teeters on edge of bankruptcy; many major projects cancelled or mothballed.

2010 Opening of Burj Khalifa, the world's tallest building.

2017 Dubai Safari park opens to public.

2018 Bluewaters Island opens, connected via bridge from Jumeirah Beach Residence.

2020 The world's tallest ferris wheel (250m), set to open in time for the World Expo.

Language

Language in Dubai is as complicated as the ethnic patchwork of people who inhabit the city. The city's official language is **Arabic**, spoken by nearly a third of the population, including local Emiratis, other Gulf Arabs and various Arabic-speaking expats from countries like Lebanon, Syria, Jordan and further afield. **Hindi** and **Urdu** are the mother tongues of many of the city's enormous number of Indian and Pakistani expats, although other Indian languages, most notably Malayalam, the native tongue of Kerala, as well as Tamil and Sinhalese (the majority language of Sri Lanka), are also spoken. Other Asian languages are also common, most notably **Tagalog**, the first language of the city's large Filipino community.

In practice, the city's most widely understood language is actually **English** (even if most speak it only as a second or third language), which serves as a link between all the city's various ethnic groups, as well as the principal language of the European expat community and the business and tourism sectors. Pretty much everyone in Dubai speaks at least a little English (ironically, even local Emiratis are now forced to revert to this foreign language in many of their everyday dealings in their own city).

Knowing the ethnic origin of the person you're speaking to is obviously the most important thing if you do attempt to strike out into a foreign tongue – speaking Arabic to an Indian taxi driver or a Filipina waitress is obviously a complete waste of time. The bottom line is that few of the people you come into contact with in Dubai will be Arabic-speakers, except in the city's Middle Eastern restaurants. And unless you're pretty fluent, trying to speak Arabic (or indeed any other language) in Dubai is mainly an exercise in diplomacy rather than a meaningful attempt to communicate, since the person you're addressing will almost certainly speak much better English than you do Arabic (or Hindi, or whatever). Having said that, there's no harm in giving it a go, and the person you're speaking to may be pleasantly entertained by your attempts to address him or her in their own language.

Useful Arabic words and phrases

Hello (formal) a'salaam alaykum (response: wa alaykum a'salaam)
Hello (informal) marhaba/ahlan wasahlan
Good morning sabah al kheer
Good evening masaa al kheer
Good night (to a man/ woman) tisbah al kher/ tisbahi al kher
Goodbye ma'assalama
Yes na'am/aiwa
No la
Please (to a man/ woman) minfadlack/ minfadlick
Excuse me afwan
Thank you shukran
You're welcome afwan
Sorry afwan
OK n'zayn
How much? bikaim?
Do you speak English? teh ki ingelezi?
I don't speak Arabic ma ah'ki arabi
I understand ana fahim (fem: ana fahma)
I don't understand ana ma fahim (fem: ana ma fahma)
My name is ... Ismi ...
What is your name? Sho ismak?
God willing! Inshallah
I'm British ana Britani
...Irish ...Irlandee
...American ...Amerikanee
...Canadian ...Canadee
...Australian ...Ostralee
...from New Zealand ...Noozeelandee
Where are you from? min wayn inta?
Where is? wayn?
in fi

near/far gareeb/ba'eed
here/there hina/hunak
open/closed maftooh/mseeker
big/small kabeer/saghir
old/new kadeem/jadeed
day/night yoom/layl
today/tomorrow al yoom/bokra
perhaps mumkin
No problem ma fi mushkila
Not possible mish mumkin
I don't speak Arabic ma'atkallam arabi (or just la arabiya)
Leave me alone! Imshi!

Numbers

1 wahid
2 ithnayn
3 theletha
4 arba'a
5 khamsa
6 sitta
7 saba'a
8 themanya
9 tissa
10 ashra
20 aishreen
30 thelatheen
40 arba'aeen
50 khamseen
100 maya
1000 elf

Food glossary

The traditional Middle Eastern meal consists of a wide selection of small dishes known as **mezze** (or *meze*) shared between a number of diners. Most or all of the following dishes, dips and other ingredients are found in the city's better Middle Eastern (or "Lebanese", as they are usually described) restaurants and cafés, although note that vagaries in the transliteration from Arabic script to English can result in considerable variations in spelling.

arayes slices of pitta bread stuffed with spiced meat and baked
baba ghanouj all-purpose dip made from grilled aubergine (eggplant) mixed with ingredients like tomato, onion, lemon juice and garlic
burghul cracked wheat, often used as an ingredient in Middle Eastern dishes such as tabbouleh
falafel deep-fried balls of crushed chickpeas mixed with spices; usually served with bread and salad
fatayer miniature triangular pastries, usually filled with either cheese or spinach
fatteh dishes containing pieces of fried or roasted bread
fattoush salad made of tomatoes, cucumber, lettuce and mint mixed up with crispy little squares of deep-fried flatbread
foul madamas smooth dip made from fava beans (*foul*) blended with lemon juice, chillis and olive oil
halloumi grilled cheese
hammour common Gulf fish which often crops up on local menus; a bit like cod
humous crushed chickpeas blended with tahini, garlic and lemon; served as a basic side dish and eaten with virtually everything, from bread and vegetables through to meat dishes
jebne white cheese
kibbeh small ovals of deep-fried minced lamb mixed with cracked wheat and spices
kushari classic Egyptian dish featuring a mix of rice, lentils, noodles, macaroni and fried onion, topped with tomato sauce
labneh thick, creamy Arabian yoghurt, often flavoured with garlic or mint
loubia salad of green beans with tomatoes and onion
moutabal a slightly creamier version of *baba ghanouj*, thickened using yoghurt or tahini
mulukhiyah soup-cum-stew with a characteristically slimy texture, made from boiled *mulukhiyah* leaves
saj Lebanese style of thin, round flatbread
saj manakish (or *mana'eesh*) pieces of *saj* sprinkled with herbs and oil – a kind of Middle Eastern mini-pizza
sambousek miniature pastries, filled with meat or cheese and then fried
sharkaseya chicken served in a creamy walnut sauce

shish taouk basic chicken kebab, with small pieces of meat grilled on a skewer and often served with garlic sauce

shisha waterpipe (also known as hubbly-bubbly). Tobacco is filtered through the glass water-container at the base of the pipe, and so is much milder (and less harmful) than normal cigarettes. Tobacco is usually available either plain or in various flavoured varieties; the best shisha cafés may have as many as twenty varieties

shwarma chicken or lamb kebabs, cut in narrow strips off a big hunk of meat roasted on a vertical spit (like the Turkish doner kebab) and served wrapped in flatbread with salad

tabbouleh finely chopped mixture of tomato, mint and cracked wheat

tahini paste made from sesame seeds

waraq aynab vine leaves stuffed with a mixture of rice and meat

zaatar a widely used seasoning made from a mixture of dried thyme (or oregano), salt and sesame seeds

zatoon olives

Glossary

abbeya black, full-length women's traditional robe

abra small boat used to ferry passengers across the Creek (see pages 29 and 110)

attar traditional perfume

bahar sea

barasti palm thatch used to construct traditional houses

bayt/bait house

burj tower

dar house

dhow generic term loosely used to describe all types of traditional wooden Arabian boat

dishdasha see *kandoura* below

Eid ul Fitr festival celebrating the end of Ramadan (see page 119)

falaj traditional irrigation technique used to water date plantations, with water drawn from deep underground and carried to its destination along tiny earthen canals

funduk hotel

ghutra men's headscarf, usually white or red-and-white check

haj pilgrimage to Mecca

hosn/hisn fort

iftar the breaking of the fast after dark during Ramadan

iqal the rope-like black cords used to keep the *ghutra* on the head (traditionally used to tie together the legs of camels to stop them running off)

jebel hill or mountain

kandoura the full-length traditional robe worn by Gulf Arabs (also known as *dishdashas*). A decorative tassel, known as the *farokha* (or *tarboush*), often hangs from the collar. A long robe, or *basht*, is sometimes worn over the *dishdasha* on formal occasions, denoting the authority of the wearer

Al Khaleej The Gulf (translated locally as the Arabian Gulf, never as the Persian Gulf)

khanjar traditional curved dagger, usually made of silver

Al Khor The Creek

majlis meeting/reception room in a traditional Arabian house; the place where local or family problems were discussed and decisions taken

mashrabiya projecting window protected by a carved wooden latticework screen – although the term is often loosely used to describe any kind of elaborately carved latticework screen, whether or not a window is also present

masjid mosque

mina port

nakheel palm tree

oud Arabian lute; also the name of a key ingredient in Arabian perfumes derived from agarwood

qasr palace or castle

qibla the direction of Mecca, usually indicated by a sign or sticker in most hotel rooms in the city (and in mosques by a recessed niche known as the mihrab)

Ramadan see page 119

shayla women's black headscarf, worn with an *abbeya*

wadi dry river bed or valley

SMALL PRINT

Publishing Information
Third edition 2019

Distribution
UK, Ireland and Europe
Apa Publications (UK) Ltd; sales@roughguides.com
United States and Canada
Ingram Publisher Services; ips@ingramcontent.com
Australia and New Zealand
Woodslane; info@woodslane.com.au
Southeast Asia
Apa Publications (SN) Pte; sales@roughguides.com
Worldwide
Apa Publications (UK) Ltd; sales@roughguides.com
Special Sales, Content Licensing and CoPublishing
Rough Guides can be purchased in bulk quantities at discounted prices. We can create special editions, personalised jackets and corporate imprints tailored to your needs. sales@roughguides.com.
roughguides.com
Printed in China by RR Donnelley Asia Printing Solutions Limited

A catalogue record for this book is available from the British Library
The publishers and authors have done their best to ensure the accuracy and currency of all the information in **Pocket Rough Guide Dubai**, however, they can accept no responsibility for any loss, injury, or inconvenience sustained by any traveller as a result of information or advice contained in the guide.

Rough Guide Credits
Author: Gavin Thomas
Updater: Klaudyna Cwynar
Editor: Siobhan Warwicker
Cartography: Ed Wright
Managing editor: Rachel Lawrence
Picture editor: Aude Vauconsant

Cover photo research: Tom Smyth
Original design: Richard Czapnik
Senior DTP coordinator: Dan May
Head of DTP and Pre-Press: Rebeka Davies

Help us update

We've gone to a lot of effort to ensure that this edition of the **Pocket Rough Guide Dubai** is accurate and up-to-date. However, things change – places get "discovered", opening hours are notoriously fickle, restaurants and rooms raise prices or lower standards. If you feel we've got it wrong or left something out, we'd like to know, and if you can remember the address, the price, the hours, the phone number, so much the better.

Please send your comments with the subject line "**Pocket Rough Guide Dubai Update**" to mail@uk.roughguides.com. We'll credit all contributions and send a copy of the next edition (or any other Rough Guide if you prefer) for the very best emails.

Photo Credits

(Key: T-top; C-centre; B-bottom; L-left; R-right)

Alamy 12/13T, 15B, 19T, 20C, 21C, 30, 31, 32, 55, 89
Antonie Robertson/One&Only Royal Mirage 78
Chris Cypert 70
Chris Cypert/Jumeirah Media Library 19B
Dreamstime.com 52
Getty Images 11B, 14B, 92
ImageBROKER/AWL Images 2BL
iStock 10, 11T, 12/13B, 13C, 16T, 18B, 38, 45, 50, 62, 72, 106/107
Jumeirah Media Library 96/97
Karol Kozlowski/AWL Images 1
Massimo Borchi/4Corners Images 22/23

Neil Corder/Four Points by Sheraton 5
Neil Scott Corder 80
Nicolas Dumont 79, 81
PhotoFVG/AWL Images 4
Public Domain 2T
Shutterstock 54, 63, 64
Tim Draper/Rough Guides 2CR, 2BR, 6, 12B, 14T, 15T, 16B, 17B, 17T, 18C, 18T, 19C, 20T, 20B, 21T, 21B, 24, 25, 28, 35, 37, 40, 41, 43, 46, 48, 49, 51, 53, 57, 58, 67, 69, 73, 75, 76, 77, 83, 85, 87, 90, 91, 93, 94

Cover: Burj Khalifa Robert Harding

Index

CONTENTS

DUBAI

Dubai is like nowhere else on the planet. Often claimed to be the world's fastest-growing city, in the past four decades it has metamorphosed from a small Gulf trading centre to become one of the world's most glamorous, spectacular and futuristic urban destinations, fuelled by a heady cocktail of petrodollars, visionary commercial acumen and naked ambition. Dubai's ability to dream – and then achieve – the impossible has ripped up expectations and rewritten the record books, as evidenced by stunning developments such as the soaring Burj Khalifa, the beautiful Burj al Arab and the vast Palm Jumeirah island. Each is a remarkable testament to the ruling sheikhs' determination to make this one of the world's essential destinations for the twenty-first century.

Sheikh Zayed Road

Modern Dubai is often seen as a panegyric to consumerist luxury: a self-indulgent haven of magical hotels, superlative restaurants and extravagantly themed shopping malls. Perhaps not surprisingly the city is often stereotyped as a vacuous consumerist fleshpot, appealing only to those with more cash than culture, although this one-eyed cliché does absolutely no justice to Dubai's beguiling contrasts and rich cultural make-up. The city's headline-grabbing mega-projects have also deflected attention from Dubai's massive but largely unappreciated role in providing the Islamic world with a model of political stability, religious tolerance and business acumen in action. In one of the world's most troubled regions this peaceful and progressive pan-Arabian global city serves as the ultimate symbol of what can be achieved. Dubai also ranks among the world's most multicultural cities, featuring a cosmopolitan cast of Emiratis, Arabs, Iranians, Indians, Filipinos and Europeans – a fascinating patchwork of peoples and languages which gives the city its uniquely varied cultural appeal.

For the visitor, there's far more to Dubai than designer boutiques and five-star hotels – although of course if all you're looking for is a luxurious dose of sun, sand and shopping, the city takes some beating. If you want to step beyond the tourist clichés, however, you'll find that Dubai has much more to offer than you might think. The old city centre serves up many fascinating reminders of Dubai's

Antique Bazaar restaurant

past, including the grand old wind-towered mansions of Bastakiya and Shindagha; the stately wooden dhows, which still moor up alongside the breezy Creek; and, of course, the helter-skelter souks of Bur Dubai and Deira, piled high with traditional Arabian jewellery, scents and spices – frankincense from Somalia, bedouin necklaces from Oman, rose leaves from Iran, and much more. The city's modern attractions are equally memorable, ranging from world-famous contemporary icons like the futuristic Burj Khalifa, the world's tallest building, and the iconic, sail-shaped Burj al Arab through to myriad quirkier attractions – kitsch faux-Arabian bazaars, ersatz pyramids, zany themed shopping malls and a string of other

Best places for a Dubai view

Dubai is the world's tallest city and getting your head in the clouds is all part of the experience. The "At the Top" tour to the stunning observation deck of the **Burj Khalifa** (see page 51) is unmissable, while the best bars for a bird's-eye view include **Neos** (see page 59), **Bar 44** (see page 80), **Vault** (see page 59) and **Up on the Tenth** (see page 41).

Spice Souk

wonderful, wacky and sometimes downright weird modern developments. In addition, Dubai is within easy striking distance of a number of other rewarding day-trip destinations, including Sharjah, home to some fine museums, the laidback inland oasis city of Al Ain and the vibrant megalopolis of Abu Dhabi, capital of the UAE.

The 2008 credit crunch hit Dubai hard, pushing the city to the verge of bankruptcy and signalling the end of some of the more extravagant mega-projects (including, for example, an artificial archipelago in the shape of the solar system and the world's biggest theme park, complete with animatronic dinosaurs and a life-sized replica of the Taj Mahal, to mention just two). Pronouncements of the city's demise proved somewhat premature, however, and Dubai remains one of the twenty-first century's most fascinating and vibrant urban experiments in progress. Visit now to see history, literally, in the making.

When to visit

The best time to visit Dubai is in the cooler winter months from December through to February, with average daily temperatures in the mid-20s °C. Temperatures rise significantly from March through to April, and in October and November, when the thermometer regularly nudges up into the 30s. From May to September the city boils – July and August are especially suffocating – with average temperatures in the high 30s to low 40s (and frequently higher). Room rates at most of the top hotels fall during this period, sometimes dramatically, making the summer an excellent time to enjoy some authentic Dubaian luxury at relatively affordable prices. Rainfall is rare for most of the year, although there are usually a few wet days during January and February.

Where to...

Shop

Shopping in Dubai takes two forms. First, there are the old-fashioned souks of **Bur Dubai**, **Karama** and especially **Deira**, for traditional items like gold and spices (not to mention designer fakes). In the souks, bargaining is the norm. Then there's the city's spectacular collection of supersized malls, packed with every consumer desirable imaginable. Head to the gargantuan **Dubai Mall** for the ultimate retail experience, while the sprawling **Mall of the Emirates** is another must-shop. More manageable retail spots are the **BurJuman**, **Mercato** and **Marina** malls and the **Wafi/Khan Murjan** complex.
OUR FAVOURITES: Gold Souk, see page 34. Khan Murjan Souk, see page 42. Dubai Mall, see page 53.

Eat

It's almost impossible not to eat well in Dubai, whatever your budget. There's inexpensive food galore in the curry houses of **Bur Dubai** and **Karama** and at the shwarma stands and Lebanese-style cafés of **Deira**, **Satwa** and elsewhere, while both home-grown and international cafés citywide provide further affordable options. Most of the more upscale restaurants are located in hotels – many of the best can be found in **Sheikh Zayed Road/Downtown Dubai**, or along the **Dubai Marina** or around the **Burj al Arab**.
OUR FAVOURITES: Antique Bazaar, see page 33. Wafi Gourmet, see page 55. Zuma, see page 58. Pai Thai, see page 69.

Drink

You won't go thirsty in Dubai, although alcohol is generally only served in hotel bars, pubs and restaurants. Many hotel bars tend to (vaguely) resemble British-style **pubs**, with pints and inexpensive counter food served, though **cocktail bars** are the norm in more upmarket places, including a number of spectacular high-rise venues in flashy skyscrapers, and more chilled-out, Arabian-style places, especially around the **Burj al Arab**, **Dubai Marina** beach and the **Palm Jumeirah**. Alcohol doesn't come cheap, although most pubs run some kind of **happy hour**. In addition, many places also host regular **ladies' nights** offering women complimentary tipples.
OUR FAVOURITES: Up on the Tenth, see page 41. Skyview Bar, see page 71.

Go out

Nightlife in Dubai takes various forms. Locals tend to hit the city's **malls**, which stay open till late and remain remarkably busy right up until midnight. Visitors usually head for **restaurants** and **bars** – many of the latter host regular live music or DJs – while it's also fun to hang out in a **shisha café**, puffing on a waterpipe. There's also a growing number of **clubs**, and although many places are mainly about pouting and posing, there are a few less pretentious venues. Cultural attractions are usually a bit thin on the ground, although things improve significantly during the Dubai jazz and film **festivals**.
OUR FAVOURITES: Zinc, see page 59. Koubba, and Silk Club, see page 71.

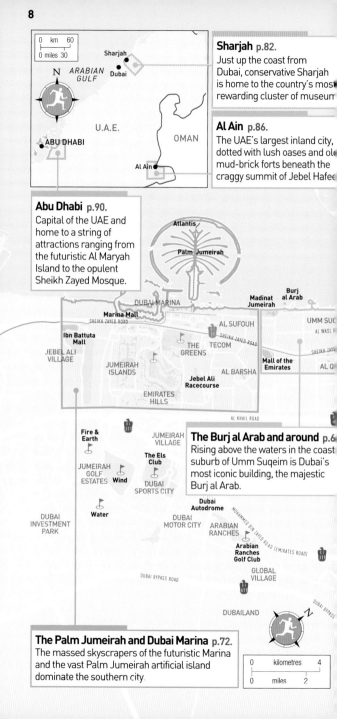

0 km 60
0 miles 30

N ARABIAN GULF

Sharjah
Dubai

U.A.E.

ABU DHABI

OMAN

Al Ain

Sharjah p.82.
Just up the coast from Dubai, conservative Sharjah is home to the country's most rewarding cluster of museum

Al Ain p.86.
The UAE's largest inland city, dotted with lush oases and old mud-brick forts beneath the craggy summit of Jebel Hafee

Abu Dhabi p.90.
Capital of the UAE and home to a string of attractions ranging from the futuristic Al Maryah Island to the opulent Sheikh Zayed Mosque.

Atlantis

Palm Jumeirah

DUBAI MARINA

Marina Mall
SHEIKH ZAYED ROAD

Ibn Battuta Mall

JEBEL ALI VILLAGE

JUMEIRAH ISLANDS

THE GREENS

AL SUFOUH
SHEIKH ZAYED ROAD

TECOM

AL BARSHA

Jebel Ali Racecourse

EMIRATES HILLS

AL KHAIL ROAD

Madinat Jumeirah

Burj al Arab

UMM SU
AL WASL

SHEIKH ZAYE
AL Q

Mall of the Emirates

Fire & Earth

JUMEIRAH VILLAGE

The Els Club

JUMEIRAH GOLF ESTATES Wind

DUBAI SPORTS CITY

Water

DUBAI INVESTMENT PARK

Dubai Autodrome

DUBAI MOTOR CITY

ARABIAN RANCHES

MOHAMMED BIN ZAYED ROAD (EMIRATES ROAD)

Arabian Ranches Golf Club

GLOBAL VILLAGE

DUBAI BYPASS ROAD

DUBAILAND

DUBAI BYPASS

The Burj al Arab and around p.6
Rising above the waters in the coast suburb of Umm Suqeim is Dubai's most iconic building, the majestic Burj al Arab.

N

0 kilometres 4
0 miles 2

The Palm Jumeirah and Dubai Marina p.72.
The massed skyscrapers of the futuristic Marina and the vast Palm Jumeirah artificial island dominate the southern city.

Dubai at a glance

ARABIAN GULF

Deira p.34.
An endless sprawl of souks piled high with everything from gold, spices and perfumes to laptops, tablets and mobile phones.

The World
(under construction)

Bur Dubai p.24.
The old heart of Dubai, with souks, mosques and traditional wind-towered houses lined up alongside the breezy Creek.

Jumeirah p.60.
One of Dubai's most exclusive suburbs, with a few low-key sights dotted among a sprawling expanse of upmarket villas.

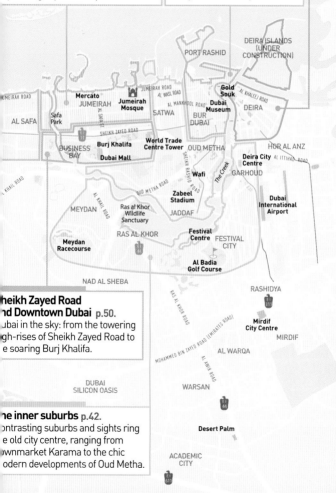

Sheikh Zayed Road and Downtown Dubai p.50.
Dubai in the sky: from the towering high-rises of Sheikh Zayed Road to the soaring Burj Khalifa.

The inner suburbs p.42.
Contrasting suburbs and sights ring the old city centre, ranging from downmarket Karama to the chic modern developments of Oud Metha.

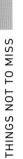

15

Things not to miss

It's not possible to see everything Dubai has to offer in one trip – and we don't suggest you try. What follows is a selective taste of the city's highlights.

< Khan Murjan Souk
See page 42
Sumptuous ersatz Arabian bazaar, with the city's best selection of craft shops.

∨ Gold Souk
See page 34
One of the cheapest places in the world to stock up on gold jewellery.

< **Ibn Battuta Mall**
See page 77
Mile-long mall themed after the journeys of Moroccan traveller Ibn Battuta.

∨ **Jumeirah Mosque**
See page 60
Dubai's most beautiful mosque – open to visitors during informative guided tours.

∧ **Dubai Museum**
See page 25
Comprehensive and enjoyable introduction to the city's history and traditional culture.

< **Sheikh Saeed al Maktoum House**
See page 29
Former home of the ruling sheikhs, now an absorbing museum.

∧ **Dhow Wharfage**
See page 35
Dozens of superb Arabian dhows moored up along the Deira creekside.

∨ **One&Only Royal Mirage**
See page 104
Dubai's most romantic hotel, with gorgeous Moorish decor and palm trees galore.

∧ Desert safaris
See page 112
Go dune-bashing in an off-road vehicle, or try your hand at sand-skiing.

< Sheikh Zayed Mosque, Abu Dhabi
See page 94
Magnificent modern mosque, with a spectacularly opulent prayer hall within.

< **Sharjah Museum of Islamic Civilization**
See page 82
State-of-the-art museum showcasing the history, arts and scientific contributions of the Islamic world.

∨ **Al Ain Oasis**
See page 86
Shady plantations of luxuriant date palms in the heart of Al Ain.

THINGS NOT TO MISS

Day One in Dubai

Deira Gold Souk. See page 34. Browse the shop windows of Deira's most famous souk, stuffed with vast quantities of gold and precious stones.

Heritage House and Al Ahmadiya School. See page 34. Catch a rare glimpse of life in old Dubai at this pair of neatly restored traditional houses.

Dhow Wharfage. See page 35. A little slice of living maritime history, with dozens of antique wooden dhows moored up alongside the Creek.

Cross the Creek by abra. See page 29. Jump on board one of these old-fashioned wooden ferries for the memorable short crossing to Bur Dubai.

Lunch. See page 32. Relax over a light lunch in the beautiful garden of the *Arabian Tea House Café*.

Bastakiya. See page 27. Get lost amid the winding alleyways and wind-towered houses of Dubai's most perfectly preserved old quarter.

Dubai Museum. See page 25. Explore the emirate's history at this enjoyable museum, housed in quaint Al Fahidi Fort – the city's oldest building.

A walk along the Creek. See page 24. Walk past the Grand Mosque and through the Textile Souk and out along the breezy creekside to Shindagha.

Sheikh Saeed al Maktoum House. See page 29. A fascinating collection of historical photographs showcases the rapidly changing face of Dubai.

Dinner. See page 33. Tuck into classic North Indian cuisine at the *Antique Bazaar*, where dancers perform nightly.

Gold Souk

Traditional dhow on the Creek

Along the Creek to Al Shindagha

Day Two in Dubai

Walk down Sheikh Zayed Road. See page 50. Start at the stunning Emirates Towers and wander south along Sheikh Zayed Road, Dubai's most flamboyantly futuristic architectural parade.

Dubai Mall. See page 53. Dive into the city's mall to end all malls, offering endless hours of retail therapy and a host of other entertainments.

At the Top, Burj Khalifa. See page 51. Ride the world's fastest elevators to the spectacular observation deck on the 124th floor of the world's tallest building.

View from the Burj Khalifa

🍴 **Lunch.** See page 55. Grab a table at the original branch of *Shakespeare & Co*, for a crêpe or sandwich among its pastel coloured, high-camp decor.

Wild Wadi. See page 65. Swim, splash and slide your way around the pools, rivers and rapids of the entertaining Wild Wadi water park.

☕ **Afternoon tea, Burj al Arab.** See page 71. Indulge in an opulent afternoon tea in the iconic, "seven-star" Burj al Arab's *Skyview Bar* or *Sahn Eddar* lounge.

Souk Madinat Jumeirah. See page 66. Walk over to the stunning Madinat Jumeirah complex, with its picture-perfect waterways and old-fashioned souk.

Souk Madinat Jumeirah

🍴 **Dinner.** See page 69. Eat a memorable meal above the Madinat waterways at the gorgeously romantic *Pai Thai*. Then head on to the picture-perfect *Bahri Bar* for a drink or two, perhaps rounded off with a visit to the city's *Kasbar* multi-level nightclub.

Pai Thai

Souks and shopping

For a taste of retail therapy, Dubai style, you'll need to explore both the city's traditional souks and its shiny modern malls.

Gold Souk. See page 34. Haggle for bangles, bracelets and necklaces at Deira's bustling Gold Souk.

Spice Souk. See page 35. Shop for Middle Eastern spices, frankincense and more at the city's photogenic Spice Souk.

Perfume Souk. See page 37. Check out the local and international scents – or make up your own bespoke fragrance.

Wafi. See page 42. One of the city's smoothest shopping experiences with one of its coolest collections of independent fashion labels.

Khan Murjan Souk. See page 42. Explore the myriad shops of the pretty Khan Murjan, bursting with Arabian scents, jewellery, textiles, furniture and much more.

Perfume Souk

🍴 **Lunch.** See page 48. The enjoyable *Khan Murjan Restaurant* serves up Middle Eastern cuisine in a good-looking outdoor courtyard.

Ibn Battuta Mall. See page 77. Catch the metro down to Dubai's most eye-catching mall, extravagantly themed after Ibn Battuta's travels.

Mall of the Emirates. See page 67. Perhaps the city's most satisfying all-in-one retail destination, with 500-odd shops to explore.

Khan Murjan dish

🍴 **Dinner.** See page 69. Have dinner at *Après*, with tasty international cuisine, crisp cocktails and fine views over surreal Ski Dubai next door.

Mall of the Emirates

Hidden Dubai

To escape the crowds, head for some of Dubai's less well-known attractions – although you'll need a car or taxi for the latter part of the day.

Naif Museum. See page 38. This little-visited museum showcases the engaging history of the Dubai police force since colonial times.

Al Wasl and Covered souks. See page 37. Walk down Al Musallah Street then dive west into the tangle of little streets and alleyways of the disorienting Al Wasl Souk.

Hindi Lane. See page 28. Take an abra across the Creek to Bur Dubai's Textile Souk, just a few steps from this entertaining little Indian enclave of Hindi Lane.

Lunch. See page 32. The lovely little *XVA Café* is close to Hindi Lane, tucked away at the back of Bastakiya.

Iranian mosques. See page 28. It's a short walk through the Textile Souk to Bur Dubai's fine pair of Iranian Shia'a mosques.

Ras al Khor Wildlife Sanctuary. See page 46. Take a taxi out to the Ras al Khor Wildlife Sanctuary, with flocks of vivid pink flamingoes incongruously framed against distant skyscrapers.

Majlis Ghorfat um al Sheif. See page 62. This picturesque old mud-brick house is incongruously marooned amid the villas of Jumeirah.

Dinner. See page 47. Grab a pavement table at the always bustling *Al Mallah* Lebanese café in the personable suburb of Satwa, a part of the city usually overlooked by tourists.

Naif Museum

Covered Souk

Iranian Mosque